Praise for Ready or Not...Here We Come!

"*Ready or Not...Here We Come!* is the advice you need in the short, funny format your sleep-deprived mind can absorb. Elizabeth Lyons tells it like it is in a laugh-out-loud look at the uncertainty, craziness, and absolute joy of your first year with twins. An absolute must-have for every mother who wishes there were two of her to keep up with the two of them."

—Lisa Earle McLeod
Author of *Forget Perfect*

"Elizabeth Lyons' humorous yet realistic perspective provides new parents of twins with a great starting point from which to embark on that all-important first year."

—Dr. Bob Covert
Leading Chicagoland neonatologist

"Elizabeth Lyons tells it like it really is. From helping you survive back-to-back feedings, living with the stereophonic crying, and coping with a double round of diaper rash, she tells you what to do, what to buy, and what to ignore. There *is* a light at the end of the Twins Tunnel, and *Ready or Not . . . Here We Come!* will help you find it. Where was Elizabeth Lyons when my twins were little?"

—Kristy Lucariello
President of *Performance in Practice*
(And mother of teenage twins)

"Elizabeth Lyons captures the universal discourse of sisterhood while guiding new mothers of twins through the first year."

—Kathy Voit, RNC
Labor and Delivery nurse

"Finally, a humor-filled, solution-packed tell-it-like-it-is guide to the first year with twins!"

—Betty Jean Young, BSN

Also by Elizabeth Lyons

Ready or Not…There We Go!
The REAL Experts' Guide to the Toddler Years with Twins

Acclaim for Ready or Not…There We Go!

"Elizabeth Lyons is the friend you always dreamed you'd meet when you found out there were twins on the way. Now she's back with a smart and funny guide to surviving on Planet of the Toddlers. Consider it a must-read."

—Ann Douglas
Author of *The Mother of All Toddler Books*

"Lyons has an endearing way of combining humor and optimism as she offers girlfriend-to-girlfriend, practical strategies to raising twin toddlers."

—Dr. Susan Warhus, OB/GYN
Author of *Countdown to Baby*

"Twins can present some unique challenges for even the most experienced parents. Lyons' witty and often hysterically funny accounts of life with twin toddlers combined with her secrets for preserving sanity reassure parents that they can survive the years with toddler twins."

—Nancy Bowers, RN, BSN, MPH
Author of *The Multiple Pregnancy Sourcebook*

"*Ready or Not . . . There We Go* gives parents the straight scoop on life with twin toddlers. Before your twins are on the go, whether you're ready or not, go get yourself a copy of this book."

—Jennifer Margulis
Editor of *Toddler: Real-Life Stories of Those Fickle, Irrational, Urgent, Tiny People We Love*

"Lyons is a smart and funny friend who offers sanity in times of crisis and confusion."

—*TWINS* magazine

READY OR NOT....
HERE WE COME!

READY OR NOT...
HERE WE COME!

The REAL Experts' Guide
to the First Year with Twins

ELIZABETH LYONS

FINN-PHYLLIS
PRESS

This book is dedicated with love and gratitude to Mollie and Barb, who convince me that I can do anything, and without whom I would be an entirely different person.

*Life is not measured by the number of breaths we take, but by the
moments that take our breath away.*
—Author Unknown

Acknowledgements

To Jack and Henry, this book could not have been written without you. For blessing us with your presence, and for giving me the opportunity each and every day to become a more patient, giving, positive person, I will forever be grateful. Just thinking of you makes my heart smile. Jack, you have been on a mission since *before* day one. Be sure to slow down and enjoy the scenery every once in a while! Henry, you are not fooling anyone; your eyes say it all.

To Grace, your ability to adapt to confusing and otherwise crazy situations will serve you well all your life. You light up every corner of my world. Thank you for never ceasing to make me laugh hysterically, especially during the moments I need to most.

To David, thank you for wrapping my hands in ice and keeping the hospital room at fifty degrees while I suffered through the magnesium sulfate days, coordinating our entire life while I was incarcerated in the hospital, muddling through nighttime feedings before schlepping off to work every day, and continuing to support every crazy idea I have and every decision I make (well, almost).

To Dr. Kristine Liberty, thank you for your contributions to this book. Thank you for being so knowledgeable and so patient.

To Allana Joy Bourne, my tireless editor, without you this book wouldn't be what it is. For your patience, candor, and brilliant suggestions, I am forever grateful.

To Mollie, what on earth would I do without you? I thank the universe every single day for allowing you to get pregnant with twins while on birth control. Thank you for being supportive all the time and for telling it like it is when necessary.

To Barb, we were most definitely each other's twin in a prior life. Thank you for the sanity-saving phone chats while we were in the hospital, and for everything since. I can't imagine my world without you in it.

Contents

The Bottom Line. . .

Courage is not afraid to weep, and she is not afraid to pray, even when she is not sure who she is praying to.

— (Makataimeshekiakiak) Black Hawk

At some point during a long night with our newborn twin boys, Jack and Henry, I sat on the floor—in the same pajamas I had been wearing for four days—and thought to myself, "It would be really nice if twins came with an operations manual!"

While I was pregnant with the boys, I read some books beautifully detailing the medical aspects of a twin pregnancy, and others laying out basic logistics for the all-important and hectic first year. Unfortunately, I could not find a book that addressed how to survive the first year with multiples in a girlfriend-to-girlfriend manner.

I wasn't looking for someone to sugarcoat the experience. I was happy to read a book written by someone honest enough to proclaim, "Honey, raising twins is hard!" Most of the books on the market communicate that very well. What frustrated me—after being reminded (again) that the experience would be hard—was waiting with baited breath for the author to say, "But here's how to make it easier (and laugh while you're doing it)." I waited, and waited, and waited.

I longed for a humorous book that told it like it is, and also gave strategies for getting through the "how it is." I hungered for an author daring enough to write, "It's true that you'll hear over and over again not to microwave formula, but it's okay if you do—provided you follow some basic rules and do some safety checks." However, after searching and searching, I realized that such a book did not exist. At that point I decided to write one.

The first year with twins is crazy, humbling, amazing, frustrating, confusing, and miraculous, and it goes by all too quickly. What initially does not seem survivable will make you laugh hysterically years later when you reminisce. I occasionally bump into a new mom of twins. I can't help but say, "Congratulations! You have such an amazing adventure ahead." Some of these women smile and say, "Thanks!" Some look at me like I'm crazy (I'm sure their pain medication is causing their confused response). Some say, with great trepidation, "Really? Gosh, I sure hope so."

Mothering a set of twins is an indescribable experience. It's already miraculous to be a mom. To bring two children into the world simultaneously, raise them as their unique selves, and watch them grow and develop into the people they are meant to be is simply astonishing. It's a hard road, but nothing worthwhile is ever easy, right?

Expectant moms of twins are too often told (frequently by people with no experience) how hard the journey is going to be. I think that's terribly sad. Of course it will be hard—some days, getting to the dry cleaners before they close is hard. The difference is, this experience will be the most rewarding kind of hard you'll ever face.

The secret to your success lies in your perspective and attitude. There will be days when you think, "Screw attitude and perspective, this sucks!" But those days will be few and far between. You will get past them, I promise.

I meet mothers of twins left and right. Many of their kids are older now, and they comment that raising twins gets more fun every year. Only about 1 percent of all the women I've met say something stupid like, "Oh, it only gets harder as they get older." I've never understood those women. Even if that *were* their perspective, what benefit does it provide either of us to communicate it?

One wise mom I met summed it up perfectly when she said, "People without twins make such a big deal out of *how* you do it. You just do it. You have a sense of humor about it as often as possible. And you take it a day, sometimes an hour, at a time."

Some people will comment that God never gives you more than you can handle, and you will respond, "Yes, but unfortunately, I think He's confused me with someone else." Then, the baby you've been praying would sleep for at least six minutes will sleep for an hour.

A finely tuned sense of humor is critical. If you don't have one, get one—fast. After all, few situations in life are true catastrophes, even though they may initially feel like they are. When you smile at or laugh at a situation, it passes almost instantly. When you cry or yell, it sticks around much longer. Yes, occasionally you'll laugh and then stoically profess, "Okay, but seriously, we have to figure this out," or not laugh at all and, instead, yell, "We need to fix this *right now!*" But if you try the former approach as often as possible, it will help tremendously. As writer Kurt Vonnegut once said, "Laughter and tears are both responses to frustration and exhaustion. I myself prefer to laugh, since there is less cleaning up to do afterward."

David, father of twin sons Jonathon and Jake, remembers, "At one point, our boys were having a particularly bad night. My wife and I were in the middle of changing the fourth diaper in one hour, plus two sets of sheets—and it was 3:00

a.m. My wife said, 'At least it cannot get any worse!' We got back in bed and our two-year-old daughter promptly walked into our room proclaiming she did not feel well. Within ten seconds, she vomited all over the four loads of freshly washed and folded laundry. All we could do was laugh. The alternative was simply too depressing!'"

Start this moment to realign your expectations. I recently heard that it takes approximately 196 hours per week to raise triplets. What's the problem with that? *There are only 168 hours in a week!* If you divide the 196 hours by three, and thereby presume that the tasks associated with each baby require approximately sixty-five hours, it could be reasonably estimated that raising twins takes approximately 130 hours per week. I'm certain that the third baby does not, in and of himself, take up the whole of those additional sixty-six hours. Therefore, I've concluded that raising twins takes somewhere between 130 and 196 hours per week. That's a lot of hours. Clearly, a few lifestyle modifications are in order.

If you are a person who needs your house to be spotless day-in and day-out, invent a twelve-step program that breaks your need for a completely clean dwelling all the time (unless you have a full-time housekeeper). I remember an evening when my husband, David, arrived home from work. I was sweating, unshowered, hungry, and unable to find Jack's pajamas that I had *just* set out. Poor guy mentioned something about a major sale on speakers he'd waited years to buy. My retort was simple and straightforward. Through clenched teeth, I said, "Money does not grow on trees and neither do housekeepers. Look at this place! Now give me some *help!*" I think I actually scared him because he didn't waste any time. He went straight for the vacuum cleaner. Whether it was my appearance or my demeanor that frightened him into action, I'm not entirely sure.

Accept that you will not dine on a gourmet meal every night unless you can afford a personal chef. In fact, there are still many nights when I find a bowl of cereal absolutely delicious, and as I mention later, I still rely heavily on the power of the multi-vitamin.

Accept that your holiday cards may not go out until March. As my husband frequently comments, "There aren't enough hours in the day or adults in this house!" If you allow it, you will have seven-mile-long to-do lists—and that's okay, provided you train yourself to prioritize three or four to-dos in a *week* instead of in a *day*, as might have been your practice in the past.

Accept that, in most cases, having uncompleted to-dos at the end of the day is not the end of the world. Most parents of twins marvel at how flexible they become. As innately organized and efficient human beings, they never would have imagined they'd choose to spend an evening watching a movie *before* they cleaned the dirty dishes. Or, that, pulling out of their driveway to go meet Santa Clause, they'd switch gears—literally—because one of the babies' diapers exploded all over her brand new Christmas outfit (the white one). For most parents, this shift in mentality is as much of a blessing as the arrival of their children. They have a newfound awareness of those truly important things in life versus the merely peripheral details.

If you weren't organized before, I guarantee you will be soon. If you *were* organized before, you're going to "kick it up a notch," as renowned chef (and father of twins) Emeril Lagasse would say.

I was unexpectedly admitted to the hospital in pre-term labor when I was thirty-two weeks pregnant, and I came home for only twenty-four hours before I went into unstoppable labor and delivered Jack and Henry at thirty-five weeks and two days. The boys were in the neonatal intensive care unit (NICU) for sixteen days before we were able to bring them home. What the boys' little vacation in the NICU gave us was the extremely positive chance to get things as ready as time permitted. But to be perfectly honest, the best way to organize is simply to live it and see what works for you. It won't be more than fifteen hours before you'll have some high-priority challenges that need solutions. Fast. And you'll come up with them just as quickly as does every other mother of multiples. Remember, you would not have been blessed with multiples if someone didn't have complete and utter confidence that you were up to the challenge.

Have empowering mantras at-the-ready. My mother-in-law taught me the mantra she invented to deal with challenging people or situations: Breathe. Smile. Love.

Breathing always helps. One, you need oxygen to live through the challenging moment. Two, deep breathing lowers your blood pressure and helps you calm down. One breathing exercise I recently learned is, take a deep breath, and on the exhale quietly say, "Ahhhh." Say it almost as a whisper. For some reason, this exercise provides a subtle release of frustration, which is helpful during moments of extreme stress.

A smile—even if forced—dulls the most agitated psyche. It sounds insane, but in your most harried moment—whether dealing with crying babies or a stranger who captures that parking spot you've waited on for five minutes—a simple smile relaxes you.

As for the Love portion of her mantra, my mother-in-law believes everything comes down to our ability to love in all circumstances. I often tell her that I simply cannot love the idiots who steal my parking spaces. She reminds me to love *myself* in those moments. Choose an approach, she says, that prevents me from losing precious moments being angry with someone who is not directing an ounce of positive energy in my direction. Point taken.

I had the good fortune of meeting seven amazing women through a Marvelous Multiples birthing class at our local hospital a few months before our babies were born. (See http://www.marvelousmultiples.com for more information on this program and to find out about local class offerings.) We hit it off as though we'd known each other in a prior life.

Together, we went through pregnancy, bed rest, and hospitalization; and, finally, parenting. The hospital staff still marvels at our group, often referring to it as the "multiples" sorority because we bonded so quickly.

There was a point when four or five members of our group were in the hospital on large amounts of drugs to stop pre-term labor. After sending our husbands to the snack room to make us yet another Sprite and cranberry juice concoction, we wondered where they were when they didn't return after twenty or thirty minutes. Turned out, they were talking football or basketball or dilation in the hall together. They got along as well as we did. That support was possibly provided for each of us early on because a higher power didn't think any of us would make it without the others. Have faith that the universe will provide what (or whom) you need to make this journey.

Barb was one of the first friends I made through the Marvelous Multiples class. I received a voice mail message from her the day after our third class.

"Hi, Liz? This is Barb. From the multiples class," she began. "I know you don't know me very well, but I'm getting conflicting information from my OB group—*our* OB group, I think we go to the same one—on the whole bed rest concept. I thought I'd see what messages you're getting. If you have a moment, would you call me back?"

I returned her call straight away. The next hour was right out of a sitcom.

"I know I'm two weeks further along than you are, but are they saying you're going to be put on bed rest?" she asked

"No. No one has said anything to me about bed rest," I replied. "What is the rationale for putting *you* on bed rest?"

"Yeah, there doesn't seem to be one," she replied, clearly miffed. "That's the real problem. Oh, and every time I waddle into their office and see a different doctor, I get different direction on whether I'm going to be put on bed rest, not to mention what bed rest really means. Do you think I should just lie down for the rest of this pregnancy? Because I don't like to lie down. I'd rather go running."

The running comment threw me. I don't run unless my daughter is headed into oncoming traffic. And given that I had a very active soon-to-be two-year-old, the idea of being forced to lie down sounded great. Barb wasn't nearly as excited about the prospect.

We discussed her possibly impending lifestyle change and its potential ramifications (no running, nothing good on TV between 1:00 and 4:00, etc.) in more depth than any two people should discuss anything so seemingly insignificant, especially given that we weren't sure it was even going to happen. We researched independently, reconvened via phone to share the findings of our research, and pretty much became each other's ongoing secondary medical consultant.

From that phone conversation on, ever so slowly, our lives began imitating each other's. Barb *did* get put on bed rest—finally all doctors in the practice agreed that it was non-negotiable; the next day I got put on bed rest. I sort of enjoyed it (my mother, who was thrust into the roles of full-time grandmother as well as mom and stand-in nurse to the couch-bound beached whale, probably didn't enjoy it quite as much).

Barb's major complaint was, "I drink so much water I have to pee every fifteen minutes, but I'm only supposed to get up once every hour or two. Which is worse, getting up every twenty minutes to pee or having my extra-full bladder either explode or cause even *more* contractions?" We spent two hours discussing that challenge because, honestly, what else were we going to do?

When I went into the hospital at thirty-two weeks in pre-term labor, I called Barb while the magnesium sulfate coursed into my system. I wanted to let her know that, should this happen to her, it wasn't that bad. But, that phone call was placed only two boluses of magnesium sulfate into the evening. (A bolus is a large dose of medication given to jumpstart the desired effect; in this case, the doctors were trying to relax my uterus so that my contractions would stop. After the bolus is completed and your body is responding properly, the medication is infused much more slowly). My body wasn't real interested in responding to the first *two* boluses, and, therefore, over the next thirty minutes or so, I required two more. After the final one, my opinion on the experience being "not that bad" had done a one-eighty, and I was nearly comatose. This was unfortunate, because two days later, Barb was right across the hall with her own magnesium sulfate drip—expecting it not to be horrible, per my reassurance, but learning the hard way that I'd spoken too soon.

Four days later, Barb's contractions became too frequent and she had to have *more* magnesium sulfate. Three hours later, so did I. By this point in our pregnancies, Barb and I had revisited our college days and once again become addicted to *Days of Our Lives* (we had to find *something* to watch between 1:00 and 4:00). The magnesium sulfate had rendered us nearly blind, and we were devastated when we couldn't visually keep up with the story line. So we listened, and chatted via phone during commercial breaks about how we *thought* the scenes might be playing out for those watching with the full spectrum of their senses intact.

To put it mildly, by the time Barb and I delivered our babies, I knew more about Barb than I did about people I've known for twenty years. We were notorious among the nursing staff for engaging in "unnecessary and unproductive" phone calls with one another at least once per day.

"Did you see the doctor yet? What did they tell you today?" she'd ask.

"You mean they came to *see* you?" I responded incredulously. "No one even came to *see* me today." We had become quite dependent on our doctors' visits as a not-to-be-missed event—an opportunity to get an update on when the babies were going to come out, when we were going to go home, or both. It was preposterous.

At one point, I had an obstetrician tell me on a Monday that I was dilated to four centimeters. On Tuesday, a different obstetrician from the same practice informed me that I was dilated to only one centimeter. I realize that a measurement of dilation is somewhat subjective, and that doctors with big hands might declare you one centimeter dilated while one with teeny fingers might declare you two centimeters dilated. But there was positively no way, in my opinion, that this kind of differential was normal.

I dialed Room 512 to give Barb my morning report. Her response: "Yeah, you know, there are a lot of things I'd research or otherwise do to help you receive clarity on an issue," she said supportively. "But this is one I ain't touching—and I mean that in every way. But hey, it' only twenty or so hours until whoever's on call tomorrow might come see you. Then you can get a tie-breaker assessment!"

When I actually delivered my babies, I told the nursing staff they might as well set up the second delivery room while they were at it because I expected Barb to show up any minute.

One particularly challenging morning when our babies were three or four weeks old, I received a "just checking in" call from Barb. We could barely hear each other. Heck was breaking loose in the background of my happy home. Jack and Henry were screaming, and I had no idea what was wrong; I had been feeding them around the clock. "Probably they are suffering from nothing more than extreme exhaustion," I thought, but while I tried to convince them that falling asleep would be easier if they'd just stop screaming, they weren't listening.

I sat Indian-style on our loveseat; Jack balanced on one knee and Henry on the other. I was trying to bottle-feed them simultaneously while waiting for one of them to do a back flip off of my knee or sit straight up and ask—in clear English—how on earth I, their mother, could not figure out how to make them happy!

"I'll tell you what," Barb said. "My mother-in-law is here. Why don't I come over and give you a hand."

"*What?*" I answered incredulously. "No. You have two babies of your own over there. I'll be fine—I think."

Too tired to argue, she replied, "Well, call me back if you pass the point of no return. I'll come right over."

I thanked her, hung up, and returned to my attempt to comfort the babies.

Fifteen minutes later, I heard a tap on the front door. "Oh, this ought to be good," I thought. "I cannot get up, I have not showered in days, and there is intense screaming going on in here." Then I saw Barb looking in through the front door sidelights. I could not believe it. I managed to get up and open the door, and she said simply, "I knew you wouldn't call."

She entered the foyer, looked around, and asked, "What exactly is the problem here?" Of course, the moment Barb walked in the door, both boys stopped crying. The only thing that saved me from being seen as a drama queen in need of major attention was the fact that she'd already heard the decibel level of their screaming. Barb stayed for about thirty minutes (the boys making nary a peep), walked out the front door, and the screaming began again. Still clueless, I prepared two more bottles, thanked the gods of true friendship, said a silent prayer to the gods of calm and quiet, and plugged the bottles into their wide-open mouths.

In the early weeks, David's and my families helped a lot, but they all lived hundreds of miles away and couldn't take up permanent residence with us. I've purchased books about getting through challenging times, only to find page twelve saying the survivor had two nannies, a plethora of family members living nearby, and a bottomless bank account. None of those luxuries applied to us.

Our neighbors kindly brought dinner four nights in a row, and I truly believe the only thing that kept several of my out-of-state friends from coming to help was their responsibility to their own children. We were on our own. It didn't make sense to waste time thinking or talking about how easy it might be if we had parents living a block away, or a live-in nanny, or a plan to clone ourselves. Our reality was our reality, and we had to find a way to make it work within the boundaries that applied to us.

Enter this adventure with your eyes wide open. Remember, you will have good days and not-so-good days. Respect and reflect often upon your blessings. Many mothers of multiples were not completely shocked to see more than one heartbeat on ultrasound (my friend Mollie, who conceived fraternal twins while on birth control, being an exception).

Mollie and I met in the Marvelous Multiples class; however, for whatever reason, we didn't get the opportunity to chat much during or after class. My friendship with Mollie began on day fifteen of my three-week-long hospital stay for pre-term labor.

After two weeks of being confined to bed, I was permitted a short wheelchair ride around the Labor and Delivery Unit. Paul and Holly's triplets were two weeks old, and they asked us to visit them in the NICU. On the way, the nurse paused in each of my incarcerated "sorority" sisters' doorways. Mollie's room was the last stop.

I looked in and saw Mollie sitting up in bed, but staring out into space. Her husband, Gary, was sitting in a chair nearby, fixated on a televised football game. Mollie didn't realize I was there, and I cautiously said, "Um, hi there!" I wasn't sure at what stage in the labor-stopping process she was, and I knew that if she was at the point I was at a week earlier, she might respond with a curt, "Hi. Get out."

But she didn't.

She looked over, and with an ear-to-ear smile so bright it was like the sun had just come out, said, "Hi! Ohmigod, *how* are you doing this?"

"How am I doing what?" I asked.

"How are you convincing them to let you out of bed?" she asked, but still with a smile that made me feel confident she didn't hate me for *being* out of bed. She genuinely wanted to know how to get them to let *her* out of bed.

It didn't take long for me to learn that Mollie is all about collecting information: What's the healthiest food to eat while pregnant with twins? What's the safest position to sleep in while pregnant with twins? I know you can't feed honey to babies under one year old, but can I eat a graham cracker if it has honey baked *into* it? And how do you get out of bed while hospitalized with twins (provided there's absolutely no chance that getting out of bed will cause any harm, or even mild disruption, to the babies)?

When she found out that she was pregnant, Mollie was terrified to tell Gary. They were not yet planning to start a family, and she was concerned about his reaction. Once she told him, he was thrilled, and they vowed they'd make it work. And then, when she was twelve weeks pregnant, she started having mild cramps. The doctor had her come to the office first thing the following morning.

The nurse wasn't able to find a heartbeat, but wasn't terribly concerned because a baby's heartbeat is sometimes not heard until around twelve weeks. To mollify her concerns, they did an in-office ultrasound.

"Okay, this baby looks just great," said the doctor. "Here's the heartbeat, here's the placenta. Looks great." Mollie and Gary were as relieved as any expectant parents would be after receiving such positive news.

"Your uterus looks normal," comforted the doctor.

"Should I be alarmed by what I felt last night?" asked Mollie.

"Well, let's talk about that in a minute," said the doctor. "I think what's happening is, you're growing very quickly, and you're feeling your ligaments stretching."

"And here's the reason you're growing quickly: there's

another one!" exclaimed the doctor.

"Another what?" asked Mollie with trepidation.

"Another baby."

Because the mood in the room had been pretty light to that point, Mollie actually thought he was joking.

"Doctor, this really isn't the time to joke," reprimanded Mollie.

"I'm quite serious," said the doctor.

"Um, okay, how do you know that's *my* uterus?" asked Mollie. Not being familiar with the way an ultrasound machine works, Mollie thought that perhaps the doctor had inadvertently pulled up the ultrasound of a woman who'd been scanned the day before.

"Because I've done this before," reassured the doctor, with an emerging grin. "I'm trained. I went to medical school for a few years." He then showed Mollie and Gary each baby's distinct sac.

Gary grabbed Mollie's hand, and Mollie honestly thought he was going to fall over backward. It took Mollie and Gary a while to acclimate to this newfound reality (in fact, Mollie claims she's still acclimating).

With the exception of Mollie, many of us resorted to whatever methods were necessary to become pregnant. We didn't find ourselves in the doctor's office saying, "Now, I'm really hoping this procedure works, Doctor, but just so you know, I'm only willing to carry 2.8 children at once." There's not a lot of time to wonder *how* you are going to do it. As that wise mother said, you just do it. You remind yourself that the challenging times will be infrequent compared with the joys, triumphs, and miracles you experience as a mother of twins.

In your darkest, most sleep-deprived moments, remember, it could be worse. In fact, "It could be worse" should be one of the sanity-saving mantras you store in your proverbial back pocket. Think of it this way: during those moments when you are dealing with two unhappy campers, there are parents dealing with newborn quadruplets, quintuplets, or sextuplets.

Have you seen the *Discovery Health* channel documentary about the couple in Pennsylvania who had a set of twins and then, three years later, after trying for "just one more," had sextuplets? The thought of a night in their home during the first few months with their babies is enough to bring anyone back to Earth for at least eight minutes.

I also got perspective the night I watched a documentary on the Denny quintuplets in California. The parents already had two young children when the quints were born, and not long thereafter the husband lost his job and, with it, his health insurance. Nevertheless, while admitting to great stress and concern over meeting daily needs, the parents commented that, at the end of very long days, having seven healthy, happy children was all that mattered. They talked about their amazing children with such joy—even when they didn't know how the next month would play out—that it was truly inspiring.

Shortly after I watched the documentary on the Denny family, my husband saw a story on the evening news about a family who had two singletons and then triplets, all with the assistance of infertility medication/procedures. Then they had natural quadruplets. The real kicker: they lived in a one-bedroom apartment. If those families can do it, I would argue that anyone can.

Whether a new mom or dad dramatically changes her or his role during weekday business hours, welcoming children into a household creates a fundamental shift in its operation. To raise our kids full-time, I chose to give up a career in corporate America. I gave up many of the friendships that came with the job but that were clearly rooted in our corporate roles. I gave up variety in my life (outside the variety that occurs each day in my home-turned-zoo), the ability to travel on a moment's notice, and the practice of eating three solid meals per day—consisting of more than Rice Krispies or Nutri-Grain bars. Although no one else seems to realize it (or care), I believe I am now far more capable of controlling corporate chaos than some of the world's most esteemed business leaders. After all, if you have multiples, you can multi-task with much greater skill than the best of them.

The truth: I have never been happier in my life. I have experienced tough hours and tough days. But the rewards are so much greater than anything I imagined. My days are crazy and my nights are way too short, but my life has more meaning than ever.

As Jenna, a mom of twin boys I connected with through e-mail, stated beautifully, "Parenting twins is not for the faint of heart. But we'll take it all: the good (the most beautiful smiles and laughs from your babies you can imagine), the bad (Want a laugh? Try arguing with your husband while hooked up to a breast pump), and the ugly (I swear, some of the poops are of biblical proportions!)."

One day, when Jack and Henry were thirteen-months-old and Grace was three, we were in the process of moving to a new house. Jack was scaling the newly unprotected fireplace of our old house; Henry was screaming because Jack was doing something "bad"; Grace was running around pretending to paint the dirty walls with at least one hundred Swiffer cloths; and some unsuspecting potential buyers were coming through the front door amidst the chaos (we hadn't sold our old house when we were forced to close on our new one).

At this moment, the "what" of what makes it all work dawned on me. It's three things (in no particular order): perspective, a sense of humor, and faith. I've already discussed perspective and a sense of humor. Regarding necessity number three, you must have faith in yourself, your spouse, your friends, your family, the universe, God, some other higher power, chocolate—whatever makes you feel confident and capable (I believe the power of chocolate is *highly* underrated).

You simply must have faith that you are meant to be these

babies' mother; that you will make it through each day; that everything happens for a reason; and that it's all just one big test you're going to pass with flying colors. Not every day, mind you, but at the end of the race, you will cross the finish line still standing.

The "multiples" sorority sisters and I have been living this whirlwind together for quite a while now. We've all had our up and down moments. We've all faced challenges, and we've all found solutions. I hope with all my heart that at least one of the many solutions we've utilized—possibly invented on-the-fly—will benefit you. I wish you supportive friends and family, restful nights, and late-starting mornings. And, of course, a cupboard full of chocolate.

Elizabeth Lyons

Top Ten Secrets to Surviving the First Year

I know God will not give me anything I can't handle; I just wish that He didn't trust me so much.

—Mother Theresa

10. Constantly remind yourself that you *will* sleep again. You will eat a full meal again while it is still warm. You will change out of your pajamas again before three o'clock in the afternoon.

9. Accept that you will make mistakes. Promise yourself that you will do the best you can, and when a strategy does not work, you will fall back, regroup, and try again. Franklin D. Roosevelt said it well: "It is common sense to take a method and try it; if it fails, admit it frankly and try another. But above all, try something!"

8. Promise your spouse that you will share your feelings, positive or negative, about the whole experience.

7. Set aside time for yourself each day—even if only ten minutes—to take a relaxing bath or shower. As the babies get older, take time to get out of the house and/or be with friends as often as possible.

6. Remind yourself how blessed you are, even when you haven't had a good night's sleep in weeks or a good meal in days. Remember, it could always be worse (really, it could!).

5. Find humor in as much of the not-so-fun stuff as you can. Sometimes, all you can do is laugh or cry, and the former is much more fun.

4. When you need to cry, cry. Advises Jeanette, mother of toddler twin boys and a newborn son, "There *will* be crying—sometimes one baby, sometimes the other baby, sometimes Mommy. And that's okay."

3. Trust yourself and your instincts no matter what. You were chosen to mother your babies for a reason.

2. Although it may be against your nature, allow yourself to lean on people. You will have many years to repay their kindness, and you will add these moments of thoughtfulness to those you cherish along with all the other special memories of this first year.

1. Keep the cupboards stocked with chocolate (or whatever other indulgence makes you happy), and splurge on a lottery ticket at least once every two months—you never know!

ONE

Before the Arrivals: Preparing the Lair

Do we really need two of everything?
                    —nearly every expectant parent of twins

This was one of the first questions my husband and I asked ourselves when we learned we were expecting twins—and we already had *one* of almost everything! The answer is: yes and no. Here's the lowdown.

BABIES' GEAR

The more alternatives, the more difficult the choice.
                              —Abbe D'Allanival

There's no doubt about it, when you have a baby, you need a lot of gear. When you have two babies at once, you need even *more*. The good news is, beyond clothing and diapers, it's not as much more as you expect.

Another piece of good news: many people assume there's a lot of necessary twin-specific gear available. Yes, there are a few items you can benefit from that you wouldn't utilize with a singleton, but not as many as you might think. Your ability to borrow equipment from friends who have singletons is much greater than it might be if you had to seek out friends who not only have baby equipment to spare, but also have twins.

The best resource in terms of what you need and what you don't is, surprise surprise, other parents of twins. It can be extremely helpful to learn which products they use, which products are absolute lifesavers, and which products they had high hopes for that didn't work at all. If you don't yet know anyone else with young twins, there are many online retailers that specialize in products for multiples. You can find them by doing a quick Google search.

I definitely believe in getting as much life out of items as possible. Therefore, I recommend forward-thinking when choosing gear for the nursery. For example, some cribs can be converted to toddler beds or full-size beds, and some rocking chairs have more future-use flexibility than others. As if you don't have enough to think about, try thinking long-term when picking out products. In two or three years, you will be thankful you did.

A quick word about new versus used gear. There's absolutely nothing wrong with borrowing as many pieces of equipment as possible, or buying them in gently used condition from garage sales, resale shops, or friends. You will not believe for how short a period of time the items will be used. Plus, the amount of money you save by borrowing or buying gently used equipment conceivably funds about 50 percent of one baby's college education!

A few precautions should be taken with this approach, however. Unless you know and are very comfortable with its previous owner, I do not recommend buying a used car seat. You have no way of knowing if it was ever in an accident and, technically, car seats should not be used once they have been involved in an accident—even only a fender-bender. To prove this point, most insurance companies cover the cost of a new car seat if a car has been involved in an accident of any magnitude.

Additionally, any time you purchase something from a garage sale, resale shop, or even one of your closest friends, check the U.S. Consumer Product Safety Commission's website (http://www.cpsc.gov) to ensure the item hasn't been recalled. If it has, you can sometimes order the part directly from the manufacturer that will render the item completely safe. Other times, it's safer to look around for another product that appears more reliable. After all, your babies are very precious cargo.

If you're lucky enough to receive two of everything at a shower, or a combination of showers, fantastic! A word of advice: don't put everything together right away. Put together only those things you're sure you will use, and keep the others (the second swing, second exersaucer, and so forth) aside. If you end up needing them, it's wonderful to have them. If not, items advertised as "new with tags" (NWT) or "new in box" (NIB) go like hotcakes on eBay. Trust me, you can always use a few dollars from an eBay sale to pay for that second pair of shoes or the fantastic outfits from an upscale boutique that you can neither live without nor afford. And by all means, keep the original packing boxes if you have the space. They will come in handy later when you go to sell all this gear. (More on the eBay project later.)

Cribs

You will ultimately need two cribs. The babies can oftentimes co-sleep in one should you choose to have them do so in the beginning, but they will soon need their own cribs to keep from sleeping on top of one another (and have the space necessary to move around). Check with your pediatrician to determine if co-sleeping your babies is safe. Their gestational age and weight at birth, among other factors, may make putting them in separate cribs from the beginning a safer choice.

If you plan for your babies to co-sleep for the first few months, you don't need to purchase two cribs right away. We purchased our second crib after our babies were born and assembled it when the boys were at a point when we knew they would soon need their own sleeping space.

Changing Table

I truly believe a changing table is an optional piece of equipment, though many moms disagree. Many women swear by changing tables because they allow you to change a baby's diaper (or entire outfit) without straining your back while bending over them on the floor. A changing table is convenient early on, and in most cases, you can buy one that coordinates with the crib. Honestly, though, I'm surprised by women who use them for longer than the first few weeks. To carry one baby to his room (which may be upstairs) every time he needs a new diaper gets tiring, and to do that with two babies is beyond tiring—in fact, it's absurd.

Several of my friends bought a changing table and kept it in the family room so they had a convenient place to store all the diaper-changing supplies, and could change the babies without hiking up fourteen steps. Another idea, if you simply must have a changing table, is to get the kind with a dresser underneath and a diaper-changing component on the top. This way, when you decide you've had it with hiking to change diapers, you simply remove the diaper-changing component and, fancy that, you have a dresser! With this approach, you won't feel the guilt that comes with eliminating an entire piece of new furniture.

Rocking Chair or Glider

This is another optional piece of equipment, albeit a nice-to-have piece. You'll need a comfortable and convenient place to rock a baby at 3:00 a.m. If you get one that's aesthetically versatile, it could conceivably find a spot in your bedroom or another room of your house once your nursery becomes a big kids' room. Or, if you get an upholstered rocking armchair, you could leave it in your children's room as a reading chair (or have it reupholstered and move it to *your* room as a reading chair) once your children get older.

Car Seats

There's no getting around the fact that you must have two infant car seats. You can either purchase the kind that snaps into a base in the car and has a handle by which to carry it, or the kind that converts from an infant to a toddler to a booster seat and stays in your car on a permanent basis.

Let me make this decision very easy for you. Get the seats that snap into the seat base and allow you to carry the babies in them. They are convenient, especially to snap into stroller seats during shopping trips, but because you have to carry two of them, they become heavier sooner than one would. Mollie kept her boys in their infant car seats until they were nearly ten months old and about seventeen pounds each, but her biceps are firmer than mine at this point.

If your babies spend any time in the NICU, a nurse from that unit will likely do a car seat check before your babies are discharged. The nurse will put each baby in his car seat and monitor his breathing for an hour or so to ensure that his positioning in the seat doesn't cause difficulty breathing. This test will be inconvenient if you have to take the larger convertible car seats out of your car, haul them inside for the test, and then reinstall them. It's easier to have the seats that you unsnap from their bases and bring into the hospital.

A final plug for infant car seats: some babies are still so small when they're ready to go home that the convertible models simply won't work. The babies need to be secure and have the straps fit appropriately on their little bodies.

Ensure that the car seats fit into your car tightly, and attend a car seat check or make an appointment at your local police or fire station to ensure the correct installation. This takes very little time and provides great peace of mind. Most police and fire stations have officers who check the installation of your car seats free of charge, and I assure you, once the officers install them, the seats are *not* coming loose. When we took our boys' infant seats to our local police station, two 250-pound officers placed a knee in each seat, pushing it down. Both were sweating profusely. They wanted those seats to be as tight and as safe as possible.

Local car seat inspections are held on an occasional basis as well. Babies "R" Us typically offers them once a quarter or so, and they are conducted by staff who know exactly how infant car seats should fit.

Swings

If you are lucky enough to receive two swings as gifts, by all means, accept them. If not, buy or borrow one and wait to see if you will need another. Frequently, one baby loves the swing and the other hates it. Or, one loves it on Monday, Wednesday, and Friday, and the other wants it Tuesday, Thursday, Saturday, and every other Sunday. Swings take up enough space (no matter how big your house might be) that it makes sense to determine if you really need two before cluttering your home any more than necessary.

We met a great couple, Holly and Paul, in our Marvelous Multiples class. Holly and Paul were expecting triplets, and I soon learned that Holly is as organized and efficient a human being as I've ever met.

On the first night of class, the instructor organized us into groups of three and asked us to introduce ourselves to one another, and share how many babies we were expecting, what we hoped to learn in the class, and any other information we felt inclined to divulge. I was grouped with Paul as well as Barb's husband, Tim.

Tim's personal introduction was brief. "I'm Tim. My wife is Barb. She's over there," he said, as he pointed to the other side of the room. "We're expecting twin girls. Barb says she's here to figure out how to do this, and I'm here to learn to do as I'm told." He said all this with absolutely no expression on his face. Having just met him, I wasn't sure whether I should laugh. I erred on the side of caution and did not.

Then it was Paul's turn. "I'm Paul!" he announced, enthusiastically. "My wife is over there." He pointed to his left. "Okay, she *was* over there." He surveyed the room and finally located his wife. "Oh, there she is. The woman in the pantsuit. Her name is Holly." He lowered his voice slightly as he pointed out, "She's a bit social." Then, almost as an afterthought, he said, "Oh, we're expecting triplet girls." Both Tim and I let out audible gasps for opposing reasons. Tim's seemed more like a "that's-a-lot-of-estrogen-in-one-house" reaction. On the other hand, my reaction most definitely reflected my slightly envious "Holy-mackerel-how-fun-are-*they*-going-to-be-to-shop-for?" mindset.

Paul was not kidding when he said Holly was "social." Before the instructor asked us to return to our seats, Holly managed to navigate the entire circuit. She was like a counter-terrorism operative surveying everyone and everything as quickly as possible: who's who, who's expecting what, who do I want to get to know better, etc. And she made all these assessments in about seven minutes.

No one in the class was prepared when the instructor asked each of us to introduce one of the people we were grouped with. The only information most of us could remember was, "She's having twins."

But not Holly.

Each time one of us paused, unable to come up with so much as the first letter of someone's name, Holly chimed in with, "That's Mollie," or "That's Bob," or "She's due on

January 15." It was mind boggling. At that time, Holly held a high position at a major consulting firm (hence the pantsuit), and clearly had her life in order.

I will never forget seeing pictures of Holly's house, all ready for her triplets, with three swings, three bouncy seats, three highchairs, and two—if not three—exersaucers lined up in the kitchen and family rooms. My first thought was, "Holly, these girls are not going to crawl *out* of your uterus and *into* the exersaucers." But she was just getting prepared. She must also have some psychic abilities because, as it turned out, all three girls loved just about everything, and I think she actually used it all.

I myself sprinted to Target one evening just before they closed because I finally had to acknowledge that, despite the fact that my family room had become a virtual obstacle course, I *had* to have two swings. My boys loved them. I lucked out and got one without six hundred bells and whistles at a reasonable price (I mean, really, they only want to swing, not learn the alphabet and the words to seventy-five songs while they're in them). The pattern even perfectly matched my family room décor. Imagine that!

Once you decide you need two, see if any friends with older kids still have a swing you can borrow (and one that has not been recalled, or that looks like it might fall apart if a doll were put into it). To my great chagrin, almost everyone I knew had borrowed from someone else. Most people in the world are, I suppose, more economical than I am—or, I should say, than I *was*. I have always preferred new things in the box, with the instructions and fabric in perfect, untouched condition. That is, until there were *two* little people to buy for.

Bouncy Seats

You are definitely going to need two of these. In fact, if you get lucky at garage sales or have a lot of generous friends, opt for four. I know several people who kept two upstairs and two downstairs (or two in the family room and two in the master bedroom if they lived in a ranch-style home), so when they went upstairs and took a shower, folded laundry, or just lay on their bed in pajamas at four o'clock in the afternoon, they had seats already there. Taking the children into your room, plugging them into the bouncies, pushing "Play" on the *Baby Mozart* video, and climbing into your own bed can make for the most enjoyable hour of the day.

I am aware of only one controversy with regard to bouncy seats: to vibrate or not to vibrate. When our daughter was born, the vibrating bouncy seats had just come on the market. A friend's husband would not allow her to get one for their newborn son because he was afraid the vibration would render the child sterile. I laughed, thought about it for six seconds, and laughed again. I don't believe any pediatricians are strongly considering this possibility, but if it concerns you, by all means check with your doctor. I used vibrating seats for Jack and Henry, and I'm crossing my fingers that they will provide us with grandchildren, should that be their choice.

Bumbo Baby Sitter

This product is pretty cool. Made of a non-toxic, low-density foam, it comfortably (and without straps) enables babies to sit upright far earlier than they are able to do so without support. It also helps them strengthen their neck and shoulder muscles. The Bumbo can be used from the point when a baby can support his own head. The official age at which the manufacturer recommends retiring the product is fourteen months, but most babies are sitting unassisted long before this point, and a fourteen-month-old is typically none too pleased to be confined to anything, so chances are the babies will give up the Bumbo long before you have to pry it away from them.

The baby's body weight alone keeps the Bumbo in place on any level surface. It's proven useful for children with special needs (in fact, the company is currently working on a larger version for special-needs children older than fourteen months), and I've even seen babies sitting in them while riding in the big part of a shopping cart! It seems somewhat absurd, but it wouldn't surprise me a bit to learn that these kids will sit through an entire shopping trip in the Bumbo, but refuse to sit in the cart seat designated for them.

A Bumbo Play Tray is also available. This tray rests snugly on top of the Bumbo seat, and provides a place to put a few toys for a baby to explore. I've seen these trays in action, and they are quite neat.

The product has been approved by pediatric and orthopedic practitioners. But, as with everything else, I checked with a good friend who is a pediatric physical therapist to see if she supports the use of this product. Her opinion is that you shouldn't put your child in this (or any other) apparatus for hours on end, but fifteen minutes here or forty-five minutes there is perfectly fine. She did note that it's imperative that your child has head control before you place him in it. You should also make sure that his shoulders don't slump forward while he's in it, which is an indication that his neck and shoulder muscles aren't yet strong enough.

Front-Pack Carriers/Slings

Front-pack carriers and slings are wonderful for several reasons. First, they allow you to carry one baby hands-free in grocery stores. Second, they allow you to carry a baby who simply *has* to be held while keeping your hands free to do something else at the same time, such as, eat!

In my experience, the only downside to front-pack carriers is that babies cannot safely be held in them until they reach approximately eight pounds. Many slings accommodate children who weigh less than that. If you opt for a front-pack carrier over a sling, you will be holding each baby on the scale with you several times a day until he or she nears the eight-pound mark. When the reading on the scale finally reaches your weight plus eight pounds, you will be so pleased that you will put that carrier on and carry that baby around in it for no other reason than because you can.

Some Internet sites that cater to expectant parents of multiples sell infant front-pack carriers that accommodate two or three babies. This is a great concept in theory, but once the babies reach more than eight pounds each, I envision you avoiding the contraption at all costs because it's simply too heavy. Also, when I need a good laugh, I envision both of my babies strapped onto me in a double front-pack carrier, and needing to get one of them out (in a hurry). I imagine myself playing an upright version of one-man Twister to accomplish this. If you think such a contraption might benefit you, by all means, give it a try. But don't say I didn't warn you!

Baby Monitor

In a home with newborns, a baby monitor seems to be as necessary as a crib. I've used them with all our children, mostly because I was terrified that I'd be so tired at 3:00 a.m., I wouldn't hear them screaming (or, perhaps, saying "Mama" for the first time at five weeks of age).

Mothers have a sixth sense when it comes to their children. They know when they are getting sick, they know when they are about to wake up, and they know when they need assistance. I've heard similar stories many times: parents are sitting on their couch enjoying a movie with the volume turned way up, when the mother suddenly interrupts with, "Wait a minute. Turn the volume down. I think I hear someone." The husband responds, "No, you don't," but turns down the volume anyway—just in case. Sure enough, four seconds later there's a peep, and someone needs a bottle or a diaper change or a mobile reactivated. The wife soaks in the glory of her talent for a moment, and then attends to the child in need.

Monitors serve their purpose. When you want to work in your basement while the babies nap on the second floor, a monitor allows you to hear them if they need you. When you want some peace while the babies sleep at night, you can watch television with the receiver on vibrate and know if the babies are making noise simply by the vibration (or, hopefully, lack thereof). If the babies initially sleep in your room, a monitor provides peace of mind when you move the babies to their own rooms, and are concerned that you might not hear them cry.

Be forewarned, however. Baby monitors are quite sensitive. They not only allow you to hear the babies cry, they allow you to hear each and every breath they take, and every miniscule sound made by each of their fingers as they move across the crib sheets. So, at a minimum, keep the volume turned down to ensure you'll hear only the noise created by a child who truly needs assistance.

Most baby monitors do the job as well as another. The only real decision to make is, do you want a listening-only device or a television-style monitor? I always thought the television-style surveillance products were overkill. However, I'll admit that, when the monitor allowed me to hear our babies talking to each other when they were eight or nine months old, I would have loved a way to observe them interacting—to be the proverbial fly on the wall, if you will. And when they turned two and started taking off their diapers during naptime and smearing the contents all over the place, I almost bought the television-style monitor to catch them in the initial stages of this daily operation.

Mollie was terrified that her neighbors would hear everything going on in her house through the monitors. Sadly, what they would have overheard would've been no more entertaining than Mollie and Gary's endless debates over when and how much the boys had last eaten, their theories on why they still seemed to be hungry and why they wouldn't sleep, and Gary's admissions of how hungry he was. I did, on occasion, hear our neighbors' monitors. But the experience was rare, and thankfully—for both our neighbors and us—we never heard anything terribly shocking.

Strollers

Stroller selection is a topic for which I have great passion. I am known in my circle as "The Stroller Queen." Why? Because I've owned *way* too many strollers. When our daughter was a toddler, I'd buy a stroller and then find an outing for which that model didn't work. So I would acquire another stroller, and on it went, until I had four or five—for one child.

Needless to say, when I became pregnant with the boys, and the topic of a new stroller came up, David said, "One. You get *one* new stroller, so choose wisely." And I did. Or so I thought.

I really gave great mind-time to this. What activities would I do most often with the kids? What would I *not* do? I decided that I would like to run with them in the evenings, take long walks outside, and maybe take them to a park on the weekend with rocky pathways that required solid wheels. I determined that the activity I would *not* do was take the babies shopping. I positively would not even entertain the idea of taking all three kids shopping at the same time.

After all that thought and even more research, I decided on a double jogging stroller as the perfect choice. Loved it. It was great for walks. It was great for the zoo and other outdoor outings. But I never ran with it (which shouldn't be shocking because I've run two, maybe three, times in my entire life). And the number of times I've taken all three of my kids to the mall would astound you. It astounds me. It's a large number. It's all about survival, and in the middle of winter in the Midwest—when you've been housebound for nearly six months—the thought of strolling through the local mall is almost as enticing as the thought of strolling through the shopping area of the Atlantis Hotel in the Bahamas.

The stores in most of the malls I visit do not accommodate a double jogging stroller (or any side-by-side double stroller). In fact most of them, specifically the baby stores, barely accommodate a single stroller (a fact that I've always found incredibly odd, but that's a topic for an entirely different book).

When the boys were about nine months old, I bought a front-back double stroller. It was one of the greatest purchases I ever made, and I never regretted it for a second. Given his declaration that I was permitted only one stroller for the boys, however, my husband almost left me when he saw it in the garage.

Since my boys were babies, the Snap 'n Go stroller, which is a lightweight stroller "shell" designed to allow a single infant car seat to be snapped into it, has come out in a double version. Many twin moms have had success with this product, though you still need another double stroller once your babies are no longer using their infant car seats. The Snap 'n Go performs nearly the same as a front-back double stroller that allows the car seats to snap into the frame, but it's significantly lighter. Get it, keep the box, and when you're finished with it, refer to my encouraging words about the profitability of selling baby products on eBay.

Side-by-side double strollers are tricky to maneuver through doorways, and the sheer width of them makes them hard to navigate, especially in a confined space. If you do run, or if you have great intentions of doing so, double jogging strollers are fantastic, and they are wonderful for walks and other outdoor excursions. They are not great for malls or other stores, however, and a video of me trying to get it into the store through the double doors could win awards on *America's Funniest Videos*.

There are front-back double strollers that accommodate infant car seats. Of those, some have a stadium-seating arrangement so the kid in back can see over the kid in front. A downside of this style is that the back seat only reclines halfway since the strollers are made with the toddler/new baby structure in mind. That's the kind I bought, but it worked because the boys were older and didn't need to be fully reclined.

With genuine twin front-back double strollers, both the front and back seats fully recline and both seats usually accept infant car seats. When your twins demand to see what is in front of them at all times, however, this type of stroller puts you at a disadvantage. You'll have an angry baby at some point because, without the stadium seating, she won't see much more than her sibling's head.

If you have friends with two children, talk with them about what has worked in their situation. Go look at strollers and think about how you are most likely to use the stroller (and I can guarantee that shopping, whether you think so now or not, will make up a *huge* percentage of your leisure time activities).

The bottom line on strollers: go with your gut—and be prepared for the fact that your gut may be wrong. In fact, come to think of it, that is a brilliant piece of advice for this entire twin thing! As with everything else during this first year, be ready to have made slight misjudgments. It's okay. You'll figure out what you need, figure out how to get it, and then you'll move on.

Pack 'n Plays

Pack 'n Plays are a great investment; however, they are not small. I recommend getting at least one, but if you aren't given two, hold off on purchasing the second one just in case you don't need it. In my mind, the only time you definitely need two is during a trip away from home (when you need one for each baby to sleep in). If this is the only time you need a second one, consider borrowing from a friend instead of making the double investment just for those outings.

I own two, but merely because I borrowed one from Barb. When I opened the trunk of my very stylish "I'm-a-mom" minivan one day, it came crashing out and tore. I had to buy her a new one, and I spent the next several months wrestling with the torn one that is an absolute beast to assemble. I knew it wasn't going to collapse even with Jack jumping in it because it was stuck in the upright position for weeks at a time; no one could figure out how to break it down!

The Pack 'n Plays with a built-in changing table and bassinet are especially handy to have around for the first few months. Both babies can nap together in your family room as long as your pediatrician has permitted them to co-sleep (but only for a little while, then it's time to teach them to sleep in their cribs—more on that later). These days, several models also come with mobiles, music, and/or vibration. You never know what kids are going to like, so just go with whatever you feel is the cutest and most functional. Your decision on how fancy it needs to be will likely be guided by whether you are buying it yourself or putting it on a registry (and praying that someone else will buy it for you).

Highchairs

Since the birth of my daughter in 1999, a wonderful piece of equipment has come on the market: the booster-type feeding seat. Not the type intended for use by a toddler, but one that reclines and can be used for a baby *or* a toddler. It's basically a highchair that straps to an adult chair so it doesn't take up extra room in your kitchen. And you can unstrap it and take it to friends' houses when you are going there for a meal, which you can't do with those huge highchairs. The best photos often emerge from lining them up in a row— sometimes there are about fourteen of them—at play outings!

Exersaucers

While still available for purchase, most pediatricians and pediatric physical therapists no longer recommend baby walkers (basically a small exersaucer on wheels). In fact, they have been proven to delay an infant's physical development—particularly in the areas of sitting, crawling, and walking. There is also concern about babies walking themselves right down a flight of stairs; I did just that when I was nine months old. The U.S. Consumer Product Safety Commission has blamed baby walkers for causing more injuries than any other children's product.

An exersaucer, on the other hand, can be a true lifesaver if the child does not spend his entire day in it. Like highchairs and swings, however, they take up loads of space. The ones with the most bells and whistles are also expensive. Follow the "gift" rule. If you are blessed enough to receive two, fantastic. Put one together and wait to assemble the other until you absolutely need it. If you don't receive two, purchase one and, if your babies are fighting over it day in and day out, you can buy or borrow another one. We had only one. By nine months, Jack merely wanted to climb in and out of it, so Henry was the only one who safely used it.

Crib Sheets

The final word on crib sheets is this: have at least two per crib. Three is better. I've heard of some moms who layer crib sheets and mattress pads two or three sets thick, so when the top sheet is dirty, they pull off the sheet and accompanying mattress pad (that has prevented the layer-two sheet from getting wet), and voilà, they have a freshly made crib. My crib mattress fit into my crib so tightly that it was a ten-minute aerobic workout just to get one mattress pad and sheet on it, so I was forced to re-sheet it each time. But I figured I could always use more exercise.

Mattress Protectors

There is a type of vinyl mattress protector that fits more like a pillowcase than a sheet. You slip the mattress into it and zip it up. This way, when you go to put on the sheet—or more importantly, take it off—the whole mattress pad does not come off with it. It's a godsend. I have only seen it at Target, but other stores likely carry it as well. Buy one for each mattress.

Bathtubs

You need only one baby bathtub, and you may not even need that, depending on how you bathe your babies. (There is a whole section on bathing in the 0-3 month chapter, so skip ahead for suggestions if you like.) You don't need a lot of "extras" with the bathtub, but drain spouts and slots to hold shampoo, washcloths, and a rinsing cup are nice. The baby bathtubs are inexpensive so it's wise to get one, but you definitely don't need two because you probably won't be able to fit two babies in the tub at the same time. I suppose I shouldn't say "definitely," but more than likely, you'll need only one. I can think of only one reason you'd need two: if you're bathing a baby in one bathtub and your husband or another adult wishes to bathe the other baby at the same time.

Boppy Pillow

Many parents expecting multiples may not think to purchase a Boppy Pillow (a firm, "U-shaped" pillow designed to assist moms with breastfeeding, assist babies with sitting up, or assist babies when they are playing) because they are often touted primarily as a breastfeeding support. But Boppy Pillows are invaluable for parents of twins. If you are breastfeeding, they provide value by holding the baby (or babies) at breast height without your having to hold the babies there yourself. (Today, holding seven pounds in one arm sounds like holding a feather; when I was raising twin babies, I assure you they did not *feel* like feathers after a twenty-minute feeding!)

For simultaneous bottle-feedings when the babies are small, have the babies lie next to each other inside the Boppy Pillow while you hold a bottle in each one's mouth. If you are feeding only one baby at a time, wrap the pillow around your waist as you would if you were breastfeeding; having that support for your arm will keep it from burning like mad when the lactic acid starts accumulating.

As the babies get larger, the pillows may help them sit up, and they are wonderful for supporting the babies as they lie on their stomachs, which helps them gain neck strength (under constant adult supervision). My husband wanted our babies' heads to be "on" as soon as possible, so he was a huge fan of strengthening their necks by putting them on their tummies, supported by the Boppy Pillows, while he entertained them to provide distraction from the extreme annoyance they felt from being on their stomachs in the first place.

Breastfeeding Pillow

If you plan to breastfeed, there are several breastfeeding pillows that moms of twins have found valuable. For more information on breastfeeding pillows moms of twins recommend, refer to the Breastfeeding section.

Feeding Helper

You are probably going to need one of these. I don't think any of us in the "multiples" sorority started out with one, but nearly all of us ended up with one. It's critical. Why? Because at some point, both your babies will need to eat at the same time, and if you are bottle-feeding, any strategies you previously developed to simultaneously accommodate them will no longer work—either because the babies are bigger, or squirmier, or because they decide at that moment that they don't want to be next to one another.

I realize that the idea of using something intangible to feed your babies might sound a bit ludicrous, if not downright cruel. In the beginning, each of us thought, "If my babies are hungry and need to be fed, I'll be there!" Sometimes, however, it is simply not possible for you to personally feed both babies at the same time for one reason or another.

There are two options for dealing with such occurrences: a bottle prop or a hands-free baby bottle. I know you're gasping, but just "hold onto your pants," as Mollie often says.

I'm not suggesting you use a prop to feed a baby so you have your hands free to type an email to the friends you left in corporate America, or to scrub the kitchen floor. I'm only suggesting that there may be times when you'll feel it doesn't require an entire village to *raise* your children, but it does require four arms (at least) to *feed* them. The bottle prop is as close as you're going to get without another adult in the house.

The baby you are propping the bottle for should be near you at all times so you know when and if she is having trouble. You can sing to her, have a foot on her foot, anything possible to reassure her that you're there. Again, it's often an "I-only-have-so-many-hands" kind of predicament. While it may be a hard lesson to learn, there are many times when a baby doesn't want *you* specifically. She wants food!

With regard to bottle props specifically, there are various models to choose from; most are advertised in twin or multiples' magazines or on Internet sites that sell products for multiples.

Many of us purchased the model called The Bottle Bundle from Little Wonders. It's like a mini Boppy Pillow, and soft to the touch. It's shaped like a "U" with an elasticized band on top to hold the bottle, and you place it on your child's chest and around the top of his shoulders to keep the formula or breast milk flowing.

Most of us quickly realized that the prop does not work well on very young babies. It often needs to be propped further with a receiving blanket or burp cloth under it to lift the bottle higher, so the baby is drinking more than air after three swallows. Many of my friends successfully used the prop with the baby in his swing (in a reclined position) because it allowed the prop to be the most upright. Having the baby in a bouncy seat often did not work because the baby was actually too reclined (or could bounce).

A newer product called the Podee Hands-Free Baby Bottle was released after my twins finished using bottles. On the day I first saw it in action, the poor woman using it was subjected to my utter and complete fascination for quite a while.

This bottle system utilizes a bottle and nipple connected by a long tube. The bottle sits on the floor and the baby sits in his stroller, car seat, bouncy seat, your arms, or anywhere else that works, and sucks on the nipple much like a pacifier. The breast milk or formula is sucked up through the tube like a straw. The bottles are designed to help reduce air intake, and because the baby is feeding in an upright position, they prevent liquid from settling in the inner ear. The Podee can also be used as a standard baby bottle if and when you desire.

Diapers

You *never* have enough diapers. Stockpile a variety of sizes before the babies are born and you won't have to worry about running out in the middle of the night during the first few months. The only real question to ask yourself up-front is, cloth or disposable? I don't yet know of a mother of twins who has used cloth diapers, but if you really want to go that route, diaper services will pick up your old diapers and deliver fresh ones once a week or so. I remember my father-in-law, a brilliant environmental engineer, asking me if I had ever considered using cloth diapers. I'd be happy to consider it, I told him, if he'd consider hopping a plane every time a kid needed a new diaper. I'm pretty sure that's when the conversation ended.

In the early months, when you'd rather not lug everyone out of the house just to stock up on diapers, try a service that Kristi, mom to Sam and Abbey, alerted me to. http://www.1800diapers.com is a convenient, cost-effective disposable diaper delivery service. They accept manufacturers coupons (you mail them in and they apply them to your account), and have free shipping as well as great prices. The diapers come right to your front door!

Another debate likely to ensue sooner than later is, which

brand of diapers is best? It's a commonly held belief that Pampers work better for girls, while Huggies work better for boys. I have found this to be true, but I know other moms who think the differentiation is ridiculous. There are also generic brand diapers, which a lot of people really like, especially after the babies are closer to a year old and don't need a diaper change every six seconds. Others say that a paper diaper is more absorbent than a generic brand diaper. You will have to test-drive the choices and see what works best for you. If you end up choosing one brand and have a whole closet filled with another, take the unwanted (and hopefully unopened) ones back to the store. More than likely they will be happy to exchange them for you.

A Feeding/Diaper Changing Log

It's essential for the first few months at least to track how much the babies are eating and how much they are producing out the other end. Most of us created a binder or clipboard with pages that had columns labeled "Time," "Ounces," and "Diaper." Each baby had his or her own colored pen, which was tied with string onto the rings of the binder. Each time a baby started eating, we entered the time, how many ounces he ate, and whether he had a wet or dirty diaper.

Barb had an excellent strategy. She had two clipboards, one for each baby. She printed one on blue paper and one on white, so the pen color didn't even matter. The only potential mishap is to lose one of the clipboards, but as long as a baby isn't lost (well, for more than a minute or two), you're doing great.

Once the babies get older and eat less frequently, you can affix a wipe-on/wipe-off board to your refrigerator. We marked feedings this way until Jack and Henry were almost eight months old, not so much because we were concerned with their intake amount in the latter months, but because we needed to know when each kid had eaten. You'd be amazed how, even at six months of age, a baby can cry, and you think, "I fed one of you thirty minutes ago, but which one of you was it?" Of course, it was usually at this same moment that I realized I hadn't changed my two-year-old's diaper in about ten hours. It can get you crazy, so just be as organized as you can be. Like they say, sometimes all you can do is laugh or cry and, well, I've preached this one before.

Diaper Bag

Most typical diaper bags on the market are not the best choice for a mother of twins. They are simply not meant to accommodate two of everything. You need a bag that can be carried hands-free and not bang against your hip and/or hang from (and then fall off) your shoulder as you push around your Cadillac-size stroller.

The "multiple" sorority's recommendation is to purchase a well-outfitted backpack, one likely meant for outdoor excursions where you need the lightest, smallest bag possible. It needs to accommodate water bottles, keys, and possibly a day's worth of other necessities. Look for one with a mesh water bottle holder on each side, where you could easily fit two bottles. Mine had another mesh holder on the back where I often stored the formula-measuring container, another set of bottles, or burp cloths (things you need in a hurry and don't have time to rifle through a bag to find). If the bag has multiple interior compartments, you can store diapers, wipes, a changing pad, some toys, and even extra clothes in case of accidents in one compartment, then smaller items such as keys in another.

When your babies get a bit older (say, around one year), a smaller, more "typical" diaper bag should work fine, if you choose to get one or acquired one as a shower gift. At that point, you won't be as concerned about needing to take half the contents of your home with you when you're only going down the street for a thirty-minute play date.

Be sure not to throw out the cute little complimentary diaper bags your obstetrician and/or the hospital might give you. They are not big enough to hold all the gear required for an outing with young twins, but they often contain valuable coupons or samples. Barb filled one with two water-filled bottles, two single-serving formula packets, diapers, wipes, and two changes of clothing. She stored it in her car in case of an emergency. That way, if—heaven forbid—she got into an accident or was heavily delayed by traffic, she didn't have to worry about further delaying a starving or wet baby.

Powdered Formula Travel Container

If you feed your babies formula, I highly recommend the purchase of two formula-measuring containers. These containers are often overlooked because they are sometimes called "Powdered Milk Containers," making their purpose somewhat unclear. Often sold near the bottles, the containers are small and divided into three or four compartments, each meant to hold one feeding's worth of powdered formula.

If you are away from home during a feeding, fill the compartments with the amount of powdered formula you will need for each feeding. If your babies are on two different formulas (which I recommend avoiding at all costs—it's just too confusing), you can measure out different formulas into each container, and mark them accordingly.

Clothing

The bottom line is, you might never feel you have enough clothing for twins. The babies' closet might be overflowing. Your husband might profess that you positively, unconditionally do *not* need another item of clothing for the babies. But five days later, you'll go into their closet to get two outfits and the racks will be empty. Why? Because you have not had time to do laundry, *or* notice that the contents of the closet have been dwindling. I am not proposing that you buy until you drop. Over time, you will get into a pattern of doing laundry more often, and that alone will solve at least 92 percent of the problem.

In the beginning, be sure you have plenty of pajamas and onesies. You should plan to acquire enough of these for between one and a half and two babies. You will go through them like you go through caffeinated beverages. From spit-up, to diaper leaks, to accidentally pouring half a glass of water down your child's front because you've fallen asleep, you're going to need a lot of the basics in the beginning to keep you from *having* to do three loads of laundry each day.

While I've become quite cost-conscious over the past few years, I can honestly say that, in the end, the added expense of a few extra basic pieces was worth it to save my sanity during the first few months. More quickly than you would believe, you'll learn how to bargain shop with the best of them to cover the next seventeen years of their lives.

Halo SleepSack

A really great product that's come out in recent years is the Halo SleepSack. It's reminiscent of the "wearable blankets" you are likely familiar with that are made of fleece and zipper up the front. But, the SleepSack is made of lightweight cotton and it's sleeveless. It carries the recommendation seal from the First Candle/SIDS alliance because it reduces the risk of a baby covering his face with a blanket and inhaling carbon dioxide.

I remember putting my newborn daughter to bed in a gown, and then putting a light blanket on her, tucking it into the sides of the mattress at least one hundred times to make sure it wasn't going to come loose. Then I'd move her closer to the foot of the bed and re-tuck the blanket out of fear that, unless her feat were at the foot of the bed, she might scoot down under the blanket. I'd then listen incessantly to the baby monitor. Each time it sounded like she was moving (even if it was only her finger moving), I'd run into her room to make sure she hadn't found her way under the blanket, or that the gown hadn't made its way up over her head. It was insane. With the arrival of the Halo SleepSack, putting a baby to sleep in a onesie—or a pair of footed pajamas if it's cooler out—and then putting him inside the SleepSack makes for easy diaper changes and far fewer worries over the baby's safety.

MAMA'S GEAR

Don't agonize. Organize.

—Florynce Kennedy

Headset Phone

This is a very important staple. During the first few months, you'll want to have conversations with other adults (possibly even telemarketers) just to keep in touch with the outside world. It's hard to do that while juggling one baby, let alone two. Invest in a headset for your current phone, or a headset phone if your current phone doesn't accommodate a headset attachment. You will be able to do whatever you would otherwise be doing, plus talk at the same time. My sister got me a headset phone as a birthday/Christmas gift the first December after our boys were born, and it was one of the best gifts I ever received.

Voice Recorder

Even before you were expecting twins, how many times did you drive down the highway and suddenly think, "Oh, I *have* to call so-and-so tonight," or instantaneously recall some piece of information you couldn't remember when you needed it three hours earlier? Then, how many times did you—let's face it, unsafely—reached over with your right hand to rummage through your purse for a pen and scrap of paper while keeping one eye on the road and your left hand on the wheel? When you have babies in the car, you really want to avoid risking a wreck while trying to find a pencil to jot down "Motley Crüe – Don't Go Away Mad (Just

Go Away).”

A wonderful product to have handy at such time is a voice recorder. Inexpensive and small, it's easy to use without having to look at it. I keep mine in my purse (or in the cup holder if I'm driving), and when I think of something I need to do, I record it. This is also a great way to quickly record a baby's first smile, first roll, first attempt at rolling over, etc. You won't always have time to go running for the baby book, and this approach ensures that you have the date (and maybe even the time) noted so that you can record it later.

My daughter thinks that each time I record something, it has to do with writing a book. Therefore, each time I play back the recordings, I can usually hear her in the background asking, “Mom, are you writing another book *again?*”

Subscriptions to Body + Soul *and* Wondertime *Magazines*

Until recently, I received so many magazines and catalogs in the mail that my husband wondered how bored I was during the day. Since having the boys, I rarely read magazines. With the exception of *Body+Soul* and *Wondertime*.

I proactively subscribed to *Body+Soul* after I poured through the first issue, delivered to me one evening by my husband. I think he was trying to support my quest to find my long lost body and discover my deeply buried soul. The magazine provides me with myriad solutions to nurturing myself in small bursts, which is good because long bursts are long gone. It's also a quick, easy-to-read publication, and it gives me all kinds of ideas for ways to calm my mind, relax my body, and condition my hair (if only I could find the time).

I became an instant fan of *Wondertime* after I saw this headline on one of its covers: “Why Your Kids *Should* Argue.” Really, who wouldn't want to know *that?* I thought there had to be a catch, but it was a brilliant article. The entire publication is devoted to finding and nurturing a child's sense of wonder, and I cannot think of a better way to spend my days than doing just that (provided the child isn't finding wonderment from an experiment that involves pooping all over my house).

Cute, Comfy Pajamas

Do yourself a favor and invest in a few of these prior to giving birth. You'll wear them a lot, and you should enjoy them and feel cute and comfy in them. When you've worn one pair for four days, you don't want to take them off to wash them if you don't have another pair handy, so have at least one other pair around that you can throw on while the first pair sits in the dirty laundry—until your husband gets so desperate he actually *does* the laundry. (And then pray he knows to separate whites from the new, never-before-washed deep reds.)

Discount stores such as T.J. Maxx or Marshalls are great places to purchase pajamas, particularly if you are still waiting for your uterus to return to pre-pregnancy size (which doesn't happen overnight), and don't want to spend a fortune on clothing until you're sure it'll fit for at least six months.

Crockpot

Oh, what a miracle to reap the benefits, prior to our boys turning eleven months old, of the fantastic Crockpot. Did you know you can use it to cook more than stew? Paella, pecan-rubbed pork, you can even use it to make stuffed peppers!

My husband got me a fabulous Crockpot recipe book a few years ago, and my mom brought hers on a visit. While the boys napped in the morning, I simply threw the ingredients in, and six to eight hours later, dinner was served. The meals were as varied as they were delicious. If you don't have a Crockpot, get one. And splurge on a recipe book or two to go with it. I am now so loyal to my Crockpot, it has its own special spot in the pantry. I still use it at least three times a week. I'm thinking of giving it a name.

Well-Stocked Supply of Take-Out Menus

There's something oh-so-nice about knowing that someone else is going to fix dinner for you, even if it costs a few extra dollars. When you've had a long week, make your Friday special by ordering pizza, Chinese take-out, or a stuffed burrito. (And, yes, I realize it may be hard to keep track of when it is Friday, since the purpose for days of the week has become completely unclear by now, at least temporarily.) Eating good-tasting comfort food prepared by someone else while wearing soft sweatpants is the best therapy available at times.

Satellite Radio

At the onset of each day, there are three things I earnestly look forward to: the prospect of a twelve-hour period when everyone is happy from beginning to end; the moment when I get to snuggle back into my warm, comfortable bed; and listening to XM Radio Channel 156 (a.k.a. *Oprah and Friends*), specifically the shows of Dr. Mehmet Oz, Gayle King, and Nate Berkus.

To be fair, I'm sure there many other fabulous hosts on this channel, but I happen to be in the car during these shows nearly every day. I've learned all kinds of ways to sustain my health by listening to Dr. Oz, including that we should all have bidets in our bathrooms, and it *is* possible to remove sugar from our diets. I'm frankly not sure how to accommodate either recommendation, but I'll continue to consider both.

Gayle King weaves a story like nobody's business. The woman tries to tell a two-minute snippet about something, and takes up an entire hour because she gets sidetracked every ten seconds or so from the original story. But—and here's where she's so amazing—she always manages to get back to the original story. I, on the other hand, get sidetracked and am gone forever! The way she tells her stories is so entertaining that it makes me miss the friends I hardly see these days a little less.

As for Nate Berkus, well, he's great on radio. He's so fun to listen to, has such a great sense of humor, and makes me *want* to redo my entire home (with bidets in every bathroom). Through him, I get to imagine the possibilities, acknowledge the realities (that it's not going to happen anytime soon), and move on. But it's fun while it lasts.

I'm also a fan of satellite radio because it has stations that play constant spa-like music. Let's face it, when the kids are screaming in the backseat, and you believe you might lose your mind at any moment, you need to choose the radio station carefully. XM radio has a station called Escape, which is perfectly named, given the effect I'm usually seeking in those moments.

Satellite radio is really about entertainment on demand, and when you're in the car with children who'd rather *not* be, it's a blessing.

Ear Plugs

When your children are simultaneously pitching fits, and you'd like to take the edge off the noise, ear plugs work wonders. When you're driving, they're a godsend (even though you look like Frankenstein with the small green nubs protruding from your ears). You can still hear, but the noise grows dull so you can drive and lose that "my-head-is-going-to-explode-with-the-next-shriek" feeling. Disposable ear plugs are inexpensive, and I keep a bag of them in the front seat console.

I find myself so distracted by screaming children while I'm driving that I have actually considered buying the Bose QuietComfort noise-reducing headphones for bona fide noise-level emergencies. I realize I'd look crazy while wearing them driving, and it might not even be legal. But if the legal issue is that you can't hear with them on, I'd ask the authorities whether it's legal for my children to scream so loudly that I can't hear. If not, what can I do about it?

Scented Candles

Very important. Why? Because a moment will arrive (probably sooner than later) when you'll think, "Is this place ever going to smell like a home-cooked meal was prepared here recently?" or "*What* do I have do to get rid of that dirty diapers odor before the doorbell rings again!" Have no fear. Yankee Candle makes the best scented candles to meet every need. The tarts, burning in a tart burner above a tea light, will fill your entire home with the smell of Spiced Pumpkin or Fresh Cut Grass or Clean Cotton, to name a few. Whether you're trying to impress guests or relax your own mind for a moment, scented candles are a great way to do it.

A Mantra (or Four)

David, father to twin boys Jake and Jonathon, noted that three months into their adventure, he and his wife, Shelly, came up with a simple phrase: "It's okay." Remembers David, "It was okay if our two-year-old daughter did not eat all her dinner, or the house hadn't been cleaned in two weeks, or we couldn't make it to our niece's birthday party, or we did not read *Curious George* four times in one night. It was okay because it was the best we could do, and we knew that. In the end, that was all that mattered."

Come up with some mantras you can refer to when necessary. "It's okay," "Breathe. Smile. Love," "It could be worse," "This too shall pass," and "Sweet mother of God, please, I *beg* of you!" are some of my favorites. Identify a few that work for you, and utilize them often.

A Sense of Humor

I've said it before and I'll say it again (and probably yet again before you reach the end of this book). A sense of humor is of *paramount* importance to successfully completing the first year with twins. If there's a moment when you can't find anything to laugh about, one will undoubtedly present itself just to keep the universe in balance.

If you find yourself terribly upset one day, still in your pajamas at four in the afternoon, your hair in a disheveled ponytail on top of your head, the house a wreck, the laundry piled to kingdom come, and feeling like your husband won't be home for days, take a deep breath. Look around you. Really look. Look at the babies, the roof over your head, the refrigerator (that hopefully has *something* in it), and the pajamas you're wearing (even if they are stretched out and smelly). Try to get perspective. It could honestly be worse. There are folks out there with none of those things.

Next, try to laugh—at the way you look, the way the house looks, and the fact that you are crying about it. In no time at all, it will be better. In no time at all, life will fall back into place. I promise.

This is the basic lowdown on gear, garb, and grace under fire. In the coming months, you will undoubtedly come up with more items and attitudes you find necessary—almost require—that might not be on this list. The list may never be complete, but at least it will help you start the adventure in comfort and style.

THE LOGISTICS OF THE LAIR

We live in a rainbow of Chaos.

—Paul Cezanne

It's likely, at some point prior to your babies' birth, that you and your spouse will decide (at least tentatively) if one of you will stay at home, either part-time or full-time, or return to work. Don't let this decision make you crazy. Your first decision does not have to be your final one. Situations and feelings change over time.

I've known plenty of women who planned to return to work six weeks postpartum. After five weeks they decided they couldn't leave their babies, and made lifestyle changes to accommodate becoming a stay-at-home mom. I've also known women who planned to stay home, and after six months in a full-time Mommy role, determined they needed to get out and do something other than parent—even if only for one or two days per week. And I've known parents who've done a switcheroo, having one work full-time for a while and then having the other take over that role.

Since Grace was born, I have been a full-time, work-from-home mom (as I always say, "I work, I just don't always get paid in currency"). But the mindsets and strategies in this book are just as valuable for moms who work outside the home. After all, *someone* has to know how to run your house, whether it's you, your husband, your mother, or your nanny. Several of my girlfriends with twins work full-time, and several of the strategies presented here are theirs.

I've noticed a bit of a debate within the twins community on whether it's easier to be a stay-at-home mom of twins (or kids, period), or work full-time outside the home. There are pros and cons to each option, but there are no perfect solutions. One thing I've found to be consistent the world over: most mothers wrestle with their lifestyle no matter what it is.

At some point, stay-at-home moms begin to feel one-dimensional. They feel they get little to no validation for their 24/7 work. They feel their lives lack variety. And if they *do* decide to get a job, even one day a week, they feel horribly guilty about needing a break from the children. They feel as though needing a break—and further, admitting it—makes them bad moms. Nothing could be further from the truth. Acknowledging what you need—whether working full-time, part-time, or not at all—and doing what you can to get it makes for a sane, happy mom. And that, in and of itself, is a *huge* benefit to your children.

Stay-at-home moms only *appear* to have more time to do laundry, cook, prepare bottles, etc. From personal experience,

I often share that being home full-time presents its fair share of challenges. There's rarely a chance to sit down and relax; and finding a balance between work, family, housework, general home-tending responsibilities, and caring for myself becomes an art in itself.

Many stay-at-home moms relish seeing their baby's first step or hearing his first word. At the same time, they envy their working friends' ability to eat a sit-down lunch each day, engage in adult conversation, and generally have more variety between eight in the morning and five at night.

I remember a conversation I had with my friend Jean who is a CPA at a major accounting firm in Chicago. Jean felt sad that she might miss some of her babies' first moments, and I felt sad that Jean had gone to a restaurant for lunch that day while I'd eaten yet another handful of M&Ms. As a full-time working mom, Jean was concerned about the milestones she might not be around to witness. I was concerned about how malnourished I might be when those same milestones were reached in my house! After our conversation, I thought, "Being home to witness all the 'firsts' is nice, but having someone else get my kids on a nap schedule and later sweat the potty training process might not be all that bad!"

Friends whose kids are cared for outside their home, or by a nanny at their home, have told me their house doesn't get as cluttered during the week, or that someone else keeps the machine well-oiled. However, these same women often feel they are missing out on what goes on at home. They struggle to fit in their corporate responsibilities with their desire to spend time with their children and tend to their home. Time for themselves is often last on the priority list. Their job requires their time, and their children need their time, and when finished with the tasks associated with each area, they are flat-out exhausted.

Some days, both the tasks of endlessly negotiating with an eight-month-old over why the fireplace is off-limits and with a subordinate who doesn't understand why his cell phone bill (consisting primarily of calls to his girlfriend in Belize) can't be charged to the company, are extremely frustrating, but for completely different reasons. At the very least, moms who spend their days negotiating with not-yet-rational children hope that one day those same children will understand and abide by the house rules and she will, therefore, feel as though she's accomplished something. (The subordinate will probably have moved on to attempting to convince his *new* boss that his cell-phone bill, now to his girlfriend in Guadalajara, is a valid business expense.)

Making Plans to Return to Work

If you plan to return to work, or believe there is a possibility—however remote—that you will return after the babies are born, begin researching childcare options early in your pregnancy. For one thing, you don't know at what point you might be put on bed rest. Some expectant mothers never are, and others are put on bed rest early on. In addition, many childcare centers have long wait lists, and you'll want to make a selection and get on the wait list as soon as you can.

Should you choose to explore a nanny service so that someone will come into your home, you'll want sufficient time to find the right service for your family and interview enough potential candidates to find the right caregiver. Feeling comfortable with the facility where you leave your children, or with the person caring for your children in your home, is paramount to engaging yourself professionally.

PREPARING YOUR MARRIAGE

The conception of two people living together for twenty-five years without having a cross word suggests a lack of spirit only to be admired in sheep.
                                        —Alan Patrick Herbert

When our twins were six months old, I had a long

discussion with Barb about husbands who don't realize the changes their wives' lives go through when they have a baby (or two). Most men continue to go to work each day while their wives give up jobs, friends, food, clean clothes, and occasionally, their sanity. Barb and I tried to help each other communicate to our respective spouses how we felt about these changes in our lives without going off the deep end (as I've already mentioned, little sleep and/or food can make one a bit cranky).

That afternoon, the newsletter from our local multiples chapter arrived. Inside was a clever summary of what I imagine many mothers of the world feel toward their spouses on any given day. Following is an excerpt, author unknown.

CLASSES FOR MEN AT OUR ADULT LEARNING CENTER

*Due to the complexity and difficulty level of their contents, each course will accept a maximum of eight participants. Topics to be discussed:

- How to fill up the ice-cube trays, step-by-step, with slide presentation.

- The toilet paper roll—do they grow on the holders? Round-table discussion.

- Is it possible to urinate using the technique of lifting the seat and avoiding the floor/walls and nearby bathtub? Group practice.

- Fundamental differences between the laundry hamper and the floor. Pictures and explanatory graphics.

- The after-dinner dishes and silverware—do they levitate and fly into the kitchen sink? Examples on video.

- Learning how to find things, starting with looking in the right place instead of turning the house upside-down while screaming. Open forum.

- Health watch—bringing her flowers is not harmful to your health. Graphics and audio tape.

- Learning to live—basic differences between mother and wife. Online class.

After I picked *myself* up off the floor, I questioned if this was a joke. Frankly, such a class could be quite valuable. I gave the piece to my husband that night, and said "Honey, in a nutshell, this is what I'm thinking many days. However, it's not quite so funny to me." It was perfect. I think he got it (as much as was possible), and the next evening he came home from work with flowers in one hand and toilet paper in the other.

Babyproofing your marriage is a popular topic these days. If you are already at home with one or more children, and will continue to stay home once your twins are born; if you transition to the role of stay-at-home mom after your twins are born, or will continue to work outside the home; or if your husband stays at home to care for the babies, one thing is certain: the overall dynamic of your marriage will change. This is not necessarily bad. It's simply something to be aware of as you transition into this new phase of your life.

Actually, a strong fear among mothers of multiples doesn't revolve around whether they will make it through each individual day. Their fear is that, when the day is over, and more specifically, when the next five thousand days are over, they and their spouses will look at one another and ask, "Who are you?" It is *extremely* important to schedule little dates now and then—even if only to walk around Target or don the doorstep of McDonald's for an inexpensive burger and fries. Even a walk around the block can restore some of your energy and give you and your spouse an opportunity to talk about your day and life in general without the constant interruption of babies in need.

Many parents of twins already have a toddler at home when their twins are born, and go out frequently prior to the twins' birth because they have a sitter or family nearby to watch the toddler. Once the babies arrive, they don't feel comfortable with the sitter caring for a toddler and two newborns. The prospect of finding, and explaining the routine to, an alternative sitter is simply too daunting, so they give up on dating for a while. Other parents initially feel confident they'll be comfortable leaving the babies with a friend or family member. Once the babies arrive, however, the parents realize they aren't comfortable with that approach, and won't be for quite some time.

I know it's daunting to find one person—let alone two—you feel comfortable leaving your little angels with. The cost of this arrangement can be even more daunting. Let me remind you of one important thing: right about now, the cost of a sitter you are comfortable with will more than likely be cheaper than the cost of a one-hour session with a reputable therapist. If you can stand it, dedicate a day to searching for a caregiver with whom you feel comfortable. She's out there; you've only got to locate her. Local family, church (especially if there are teenagers who work in the church nursery), nurses from the hospital at which you delivered, reputable nanny services, and recommended neighborhood sitters provide a great starting point. Occasionally, you'll find two friends in the neighborhood or at church who love to babysit together. This option may make you more comfortable since each child will have someone's full attention while you and your spouse are away.

Throughout the first few months with your babies, it's critical to stay aware of how important it is to spend time with your spouse. And the two of you need to engage in activities other than diaper duty and bottle washing. (I realize that certain "activities" are likely to be deemed off limits for quite some time, which I wholeheartedly understand!)

If you can get out for a date now and then, even if it's only a trip to Target to pick up diapers, take advantage of it. You'll quickly realize the luxury of having a conversation in the car without anyone screaming in the backseat. Remember, you don't have to leave the country, and you don't have to be away all night. It may sound absurd now, but once you've been shoulder-deep in Twinland for a couple of months, simply sitting in the car in the driveway with your spouse, playing a game of Yahtzee, or listening to a good CD might feel like heaven.

If you can't leave the house (and I understand this reality because it took us time to find a sitter we were comfortable with), don't neglect the many ways you can spend time together. Continue to nurture the emotional connection between you and your spouse.

Ways to Connect with Your Spouse

Board Games—New and Old

David and I loved to play Scrabble while I was pregnant with our boys. Many nights after their birth, we'd sit on the couch with a baby on either side of us and a Scrabble board in the middle.

There are so many great games on the market these days that I've no doubt you can find two or three you and your spouse enjoy together. (I don't recommend anything that requires too much thinking, since you may be too tired to think some nights. For example, Trivial Pursuit was banned in our house. It still is.)

Movies

I realize this suggestion is somewhat obvious, however, many nights, once we got the babies to bed, I quickly retreated to my own bed to watch a sitcom while David camped out on the family room couch in front of a football game or his o'mighty Xbox.

You won't make it to an actual movie theater with the frequency you once did, and now that there are monthly movie subscription services where up to three movies are mailed to your home at a time, a movie-watching evening is easy and convenient. Note: comedy works best at this stage. Sagas like *Gandhi*, while fascinating, should wait until the babies are a bit older (and sleeping longer).

Dinner

Another obvious couple activity. We all have to eat, right? Problem is, many nights when retreating to our bedroom to watch a sitcom, I took a bowl of cereal with me. David usually had a liquid dinner in front of the tube, if you know what I mean.

Order take-out, and eat it together once the babies are in bed. It will give you time to chat with your spouse, and afterward you can even play a game or watch a movie!

Designate Time

A surefire way to ensure that you and your spouse connect each day is to schedule time for it. Honestly, before having kids, someone told me that, once we started a family, my husband and I would have to schedule sex. I couldn't fathom it then. Many years later, I'm telling you, that person was all-knowing.

Once your kids are in bed or under the watchful eye of another adult, it's easy to go to the store, head off to bed (alone), or lock yourself in the closet for ten minutes of quiet time. In fact, it's so easy that, if you aren't careful, you'll find yourself doing one (or more) of the above each and every night. On the other hand, you'll be surprised how helpful ten to fifteen minutes of conversation per night can be. Even if the conversation consists of, "How was your day? Good? Great. Goodnight," it keeps the lines of communication open. With any luck, the conversation will be a bit longer. Discuss you and/or your husband's job, where to vacation when you decide you can embark on such an adventure, and the strategy for that evening's nighttime feedings.

At the end of the day (literally), what's most important—critical, in fact—is that you proactively nurture and maintain your connection with your spouse. The lines of communication between you need to be wide open. Many changes in your lifestyle will occur over the next few years, and it's easier to work through them if you keep the lines of communication open and your emotional connection intact.

PREPARING YOURSELF MENTALLY

A mind troubled by doubt cannot focus on the course to victory.
—Arthur Golden, *Memoirs of a Geisha*

One pattern I've observed in recent years is, regardless of what age a woman first has children; regardless of which of her friends had children before she did; regardless of what she's witnessed while shopping in Target or the local grocery store—after which she professed she would *"never* be *that* mom"*; regardless of what books and experts warn regarding tantrums, sleeplessness, and biting; every women believes her family will be different.

Every woman believes she will be a "different" kind of mother—she'll never lose her cool, she'll never resort to putting a frozen PB&J into her child's lunch to thaw between breakfast and lunch, and she'll never, *ever* drive a minivan. Every woman believes her children will be the exception: they'll never flip out in the middle of the department store, throw their food across a crowded restaurant, or angrily profess, "because I said so, Mom" after being introduced to the new preschool teacher.

Every woman believes she and her husband will continue to have the exact same relationship they've always had with little to no extra effort. They believe the simple act of dining out—not to mention traveling—will be just as easy with a little bundle in tow.

Expectant parents of twins are no exception. The only difference is that their perspective involves two babies instead of one. But then again, there are also two parents. Therefore, many expectant parents of twins assume that—in the area of dining out, for example—they'll slide into a corner table at the local bistro and effortlessly each arm themselves with a baby, a burp cloth, a pacifier, and an extensive wine menu. And they assume that every other moment of their lives will continue to operate seamlessly—with minor tweaks. The reality that presents itself shortly before or after the babies are born is, therefore, a rather large shock.

Let's begin with the fact that a woman expecting a baby does expand. Women expecting twins, however, often expand past the point they believe they *can* expand. I remember the first time I caught a glimpse of my still-expecting profile in the mirror at the hospital. I had been confined to my oh-so-comfortable bed on wheels for two and a half weeks, and, while I knew the babies had grown, I was not prepared for just how much *I* had grown. I remember doing a double-take and stammering, "Wh— Wh— What happened? And where did those stretch marks come from?"

After fantasizing a pregnancy where she saunters down Fifth Avenue in her trendy Liz Lange maternity wear and Manolo Blahnik strappy stilettos like Carrie Bradshaw from *Sex in the City*, the expectant mom of twins finds herself fitting into little more than her husband's T-shirts, and unable to saunter anywhere. In fact, she's likely been relegated to her couch for 95 percent of the day. The "this-wasn't-exactly-what-I-had-in-mind" mindset can make its appearance long before the babies have kept a new mom awake for three days straight.

Once it's time for the babies to be born, more moms of multiples undergo delivery via Cesarean section than do mothers of singletons. (By the way, have you noticed that "singleton" is a vocabulary word seemingly reserved only for mothers of multiples? Talk to any mother of a singleton about the fact that she *has* a singleton, and she will, with the horrified tone of a mother whose child has just been called an alien, ask, "Singleton? What singleton? I have a baby, didn't you notice? What the heck is a singleton?") C-sections require substantial additional recovery time over vaginal deliveries, and for some women who planned and hoped for a vaginal delivery in which they were active participants, a C-section feels like an unnatural and disappointing way to bring their babies into the world.

In many cases, multiples, especially premature multiples, require a short (or not so short) stay in the NICU. A mom with newborn babies in intensive care is usually challenged by the physical and emotional reality of plodding to the NICU— possibly to watch her babies through the windows of their isolettes if she can't hold them. She may feel she can't bond with her children if they can't be touched.

If one baby is sicker than the other, mom may struggle to bond with the ill baby, or she may have stronger, more protective feelings for the sick baby over the one doing better. Feeling this difference in emotions toward her children may cause mom to feel very guilty. The bottom line is, the reality of the situation simply doesn't match her fantasy of giving birth and donning soft, wonderful pajamas, and lying in her recovery room with two little angels sleeping soundly in her arms.

For a mother intent on breastfeeding her babies, the inability to do so in the initial days may be devastating if only one baby can nurse right away, or if both babies are fed via nasogastric (NG) tubes or cannot simultaneously suck, swallow, and breathe (an instinct required to breast- or bottle-feed but not developed until approximately thirty-four weeks gestation).

The mother who pumps her milk until her babies can breastfeed might feel like a round-the-clock cow. At the same time, she could be missing the bonding experience of nursing her babies. If breastfeeding is possible, the new mom may become frustrated by the challenges that nursing a premature baby can bring. And, in the midst of these breastfeeding challenges, pressure from a spouse or other family member may put the poor woman right over the edge. Sometimes the pressure comes in the form of "Why don't you just give up and give them a bottle?" This is very discouraging to a new mom, and may be terminal for her breastfeeding efforts, especially if she is already struggling with it.

Once they bring their babies home, whether a few days, a few weeks, or a few months post delivery, new moms of multiples can feel challenged by the onslaught of activity: double-duty diaper changes, bottles galore, leaking breasts, and three-day-old dirty dishes in the sink. They might be anxious about bonding with two babies, feeling they can't give either their full attention for more than seven seconds at a time. If there's a toddler or older child at home, they may worry about that child feeling left out. The excessive workload of caring for two babies, or two babies plus their siblings, can quickly exhaust a new mother, mentally and physically.

Whether they gave birth vaginally or via C-section, new moms are tired, sore, unsure of themselves, and a little cranky. Or a lot cranky. Or cranky and weepy. Or cranky, weepy, and wanting a break—maybe a big break— from Mommyland.

At one point or another, almost all new mothers wonder exactly which of these feelings are normal and which are not. Even worse, a new mom worries that her feelings make her a "bad mommy," and that can make her feel even more weepy. Add to all this the likelihood that she worked really, really hard to conceive these babies in the first place, and you've potentially got a woman with all the above feelings plus tremendous guilt for having these feelings. In fact, mothers who conceived multiples after infertility treatment may have a higher incidence of postpartum depression than those who conceived spontaneously.[1]

Let's start with the most important fact of all: a woman with any or all these feelings is *not* a "bad" mommy. She is a *normal* tired, overwhelmed mommy making multiple mental shifts as she goes through tremendous physical, emotional, and logistical changes.

Important point number two: I understand that most women have a vision of their deliveries. Some actually want a C-section for one reason or another. I certainly had my own wishes and fantasies (though they did not involve an elective C-section!). In the end, the goal is to get the babies safely into the world via the method deemed most appropriate by a woman's doctor. But it is perfectly acceptable to be disappointed, and to express that disappointment, if the delivery doesn't proceed as planned.

Point number three: the above possibilities regarding the way a new mom may feel, based on a variety of potential circumstances, are not meant to make you nervous or scare you half to death. Most women experience some portion of these events and feelings, and they work their way through them minute by minute. My purpose in detailing them is merely to communicate that they are normal emotional responses for a new mom of twins, and to help you understand that if you feel any of them, you are not alone.

That said, it's important to know what feelings are okay to attempt to deal with on your own and when you need to seek outside assistance. For example, postpartum depression (PPD) is not a regularly covered topic in Lamaze classes, at least not extensively. It also isn't routinely discussed between an obstetrician and her patients prior to the birth of a child. When I was expecting our boys, none of my doctors mentioned it. Even when I returned to my obstetrician's office for my six-week postpartum checkup and mentioned my exhaustion and the feelings coming with it, my doctor (walking out the door without even a glance in my direction) said it was a normal part of becoming a mother and would pass.

PPD, in fact, seems a culturally taboo topic. Many people are surprised to learn that this illness, which can begin as the often-heard-about "baby blues" and last for up to two years after delivery, occurs more often than pre-eclampsia, gestational diabetes, and preterm labor—all common pregnancy-related challenges.

Experts have pinpointed hormonal imbalance as the primary cause of PPD. This makes mothers of multiples particularly susceptible to it; the volume of hormones coursing through her body both during and directly after pregnancy is higher than it is in women carrying a singleton. In fact, a study conducted in the early 1970s found that mothers of twins were more vulnerable to depression than mothers of singletons.[2] Women with a family history of PPD or a personal history of depression are also at higher risk for developing the condition.

The first three months postpartum has been identified as the most vulnerable period for mothers of twins.[3] Recovering from a challenging pregnancy and/or delivery, having babies who require extra care, and undertaking the responsibility of simultaneously caring for and bonding with more than one newborn, among other challenges, imposes a high stress level on most new moms of multiples.

Another study conducted by Marcia Ellison, Ph.D. and Janet Hall, M.D. from Massachusetts General Hospital and Harvard Medical School, in which forty-two mothers (twenty-nine mothers of multiple birth children and thirteen mothers of singletons) were surveyed, indicated eight core domains of quality of life that are most impacted by multiple births.

These areas are: social stigma (feeling judged by strangers and/or family and friends), pregnancy and neonatal losses, marital satisfaction, children's health, meeting family needs, parenting stress, maternal depression, and the infertility treatment experience. The social stigma challenge is one that a mom of multiples quickly learns to deal with. Every time she leaves the house, the new mom of multiples hears questions and comments (and even judgments) about her babies—and their personal nature can be astounding!

There *is* a difference between the baby blues and true-blue (no pun intended) postpartum depression. Once a woman wonders which one she's suffering from, it's easy for her to become even more bewildered. Who can she talk to about her concerns?

A woman with strong feelings of sadness in the weeks or months following the birth of her children may be afraid to ask her friends if they've ever felt the same way. She may not be altogether sure they'd admit it if they did. The bottom line: she feels alone. And that's *not* a good way for a woman to feel when working her way through this huge period of change— whether she's experiencing typical baby blues or heading into true postpartum depression.

The baby blues is a hormonal condition typically occurring two to three weeks after a baby is born. Professionals estimate that up to 85 percent of all mothers experience the baby blues to a certain degree. In the initial days and weeks after their babies' birth, adrenaline and excitement keep new moms going. But once the initial excitement wears off, their husbands return to work, their families return home, and they're *still* dealing with the babies' crying, their own uncertainly, and the reality of a completely altered lifestyle, that joy can turn to sadness. Most of the time, these feelings subside within two to three weeks. It may take longer for moms of multiples for many of the reasons noted above.

In contrast, PPD lasts longer than the two to three weeks following birth. In fact, PPD can develop anytime up until the babies are one year old. Statistically, clinical PPD occurs in 10 to 15 percent of new mothers. Keep in mind, however, that these are *reported* cases. Actual cases are likely higher.

Bari's story

I was put on bed rest when I was twenty-three weeks and six days pregnant with my twins. There was discussion of postpartum depression in the prenatal class that my husband and I attended, however, I didn't make it to those particular classes because I was in the hospital! Thankfully, my husband continued to attend, and he brought me the materials each week.

Our babies were born at thirty-five weeks and two days gestation. They stayed in the NICU for twelve days while they overcame some minor breathing and eating issues. During this time, my mom asked me on occasion how I was doing. Because a friend of hers had recently shared her own struggle with PPD, the condition was on her mind, and she reminded me to be aware of the signs. I assumed that, since I had gotten through the first twelve days with no problem, I was in the clear.

My husband, Kevin, and I were completely exhausted from going back and forth to the hospital to visit the babies. Because I was getting up every few hours throughout the night to pump, I wasn't able to enjoy a solid eight hours of sleep each night before the babies came home. In addition, having to get dressed, go to the hospital, and sit in a chair while tending to the babies all day was tough. We thought it would be easier once we could bring them home. However, we weren't prepared for the reality of being responsible for their care 24/7.

Everyone says that the minute your babies are born you will feel a bone-crushing love like you've never felt. They say it's amazing how much you can love someone so immediately. I didn't feel that way. And not feeling that way made me feel awful and evil and undeserving of these two little people. I wondered, "What might happen if I never love them like that? What if I am the only mom who doesn't ever love them that way?" I didn't know who they were and they didn't know who I was. What I did know from the get-go was that they were preventing me from sleeping and feeling I had any sort of life. I was terrified that I'd never get past those feelings or the reality that presents itself with a newborn (or two, in this case) in the house.

I don't remember exactly when my more serious symptoms of depression started, but it was probably within a week of the babies coming home. One day I started crying, but I had absolutely no idea why. A friend of ours had come over to meet the babies. I was very excited to have a visitor, and yet every time I tried to head downstairs, I started to cry. Over and over I pulled myself together, calmed down, walked out of our bedroom, and started to cry again.

I believe this saga lasted for twenty or thirty minutes. My babies were a bit fussy downstairs. Part of the reason I couldn't get myself under control was the knowledge that I couldn't go to them because *I* was too upset. I worried, "How awful a mother am I?"

I finally called Kevin upstairs and told him I couldn't go downstairs to visit with our friend because I couldn't stop crying. When he asked me why I hadn't called him sooner, I told him that I assumed he was going to ask me why I was crying; the truth was that I didn't have a reason. He told me that I didn't have to have a reason. Thank goodness he had paid attention in class!

My parents gave Kevin and me the gift of a nanny for two weeks once the babies came home. For the first three days she came during the day, and for the remainder of those two weeks she came at night. While she was there during the day, I spent most of the time lying on my bed crying. I tried so hard not to cry, but that only seemed to make it worse. Slowly, over time, I came to realize that I was crying because I felt my life was miserable and that nothing could be worse. And then it *did* get worse because I felt I couldn't possibly be a worse person for feeling the way I felt! After all, we worked so hard to get pregnant. I was on bed rest for eleven weeks—seven of them in the hospital—trying to keep the babies inside of me for as long as possible.

And yet here I was, at a point where I was actually trying to figure out a way I could have them go back to the NICU—even just for a few days—so I could have some freedom again. And get some sleep. And stop crying.

My first postpartum doctor's visit was a few days after my crying episodes began. After I explained my symptoms and concerns to my doctor, he asked if I was sleeping, getting dressed every day, and doing what needed to be done for the babies. I answered, "Yes" and he responded by saying, "Then it's just a case of the baby blues." I felt as though it was more than that.

A few days later I stood in my closet and thought, "Today my babies are three weeks and one day old. Tomorrow they'll be three weeks and two days old." And so on. Time was moving like molasses, and I feared it would continue that way forever. "How," I wondered, "will I ever survive this?"

I thought, "This was the worst decision Kevin and I ever made." I felt as though my life was over. I was convinced that I would never again leave my house, go out with friends, get a full night's sleep, or have my own life. I absolutely could not remember or focus on the fact that it was just a temporary phase.

I went to my first mothers of twins and triplets club meeting when my babies were four weeks old. New members were asked to stand up, introduce themselves, and mention how old their babies were. There was a collective gasp when I said mine were four weeks old. Everyone congratulated me on getting out of the house, and all the while I was thinking, "Please let me make it through this meeting without breaking down and sobbing." I expressed frustration to another mom over the fact that I hadn't been able to shower that day. She responded by saying, "Ahhh, you don't need to shower." That comment almost tipped me over the edge. I was near tears as I thought, "But, I do. I *do* need to shower. Why does everyone keep telling me that I don't?"

I became irrational to the point that I decided no one's life could possibly be any worse than mine—not if they had been diagnosed with cancer, not if they just lost a friend to a dreadful illness, and not if their parent had just been in a horrible car accident. I believed none of those things was worse than what I was going through. And the craziest part of it all is, no one even today can tell me that a woman is in a good place when she thinks having healthy newborn twins is a worse fate than having cancer or losing a friend in a car accident. But yet, because I didn't have feelings of wanting to do harm to myself or to my children, and because I could technically meet their needs each day, it was quite difficult to find the support I needed from my obstetrician. The conversation that ensued when I mentioned my feelings to my doctor was far too short. It was too easy for the doctor to assume that, by asking two questions, he knew what I was dealing with.

Postpartum depression isn't black and white; there are many shades of grey. But once the doctor said, "It's just the baby blues," I assumed it was. It never occurred to me to bring it up again with him or make an appointment to discuss it with another doctor.

Then my mom took me out to lunch one day and asked me how I was doing. She looked straight into my eyes and said, "You don't want to be a mom right now, do you?" I started to cry and confirmed, "No, I don't." It felt like an awful admission, but it also felt so freeing to admit it out loud.

I am also thankful that I had a few good friends who I called every day and who assured me that everything would get better. One girlfriend said, "It's going to get better so gradually that one day you'll wake up and think, 'Ya know? This isn't so bad. I think I have a handle on it.'" She was right. That's exactly what happened—but not for a while.

What I truly wish is that one person had said to me, "By the way, once these babies come, you might not feel that it's all happiness and roses as you expected. In fact, you might feel that it's light years away from happiness and roses." Just *one* person. Had that been the case, I think that, in the midst of it all, I would have been better able to accept and acknowledge that I wasn't the only person on Earth who had ever felt that way. But no one ever talks about this part of it. No one wants to admit it if this is how they feel.

Brooke Shields' appearance on Oprah to promote *Down Came the Rain*, her book documenting her struggle with PPD, was a blessing. Even the controversy that followed, involving Tom Cruise's opinions on the matter, were a blessing because they made PPD an open book, brought it out into the open, and made it part of the dialogue.

As the babies started sleeping longer, I started feeling better. As friends showed me ways to get out of the house with my kids, I started feeling even better. As the babies started responding to us and smiling, I felt a *lot* better. There were suddenly days when I only cried twice. Then once. Then not at all. I was fortunate to have a tremendously supportive and understanding husband, mother, and mother-in-law. I had and still do have wonderful friends, and for that I am forever grateful.

I wouldn't trade my kids for anything in the world. That bone-crushing love did eventually come. They are amazing, and I am so lucky to be their mom. I love them more than my own life, and I can't imagine life without them.

If you are having any feelings you aren't comfortable with, please find someone to talk to. Find a friend, a doctor, a family member, or a therapist. These feelings are nothing to be ashamed of, and there is plenty of help available.

Many assume that the baby blues simply makes a woman weepy and cranky for a few weeks or months postpartum. Many also assume that true or "clinical" PPD isn't present unless a woman wants to harm herself or her children, or is completely unable to care for herself and her children on a daily basis. Many, many women suffer with a condition somewhere in between these two phenomena, and that can be the most troublesome situation. When you don't fit neatly into a category, it can be much more difficult to find support.

The symptoms of clinical PPD don't fit neatly into a box. Even if you are told that the discomfort you have will pass, it is more than okay to need, want, and deserve assistance of some sort until it does.

Which Postpartum Symptoms are Normal?

- Bouts of crying (even if you don't always understand the cause)

- Exhaustion
- Insomnia
- Feelings of irritation

To be honest, I don't think I've known a mother who hasn't experienced the above symptoms in the first few weeks or months with her new baby. When mothering multiples, the above symptoms typically occur simultaneously. Let me explain. You are crying (for reasons known or unknown), and then you get tired (for reasons known and obvious).

You experience insomnia when you are lying awake at 3:00 a.m. because you *know* a baby is going to wake up to eat any minute. Of course, the house stays quiet until 4:00 a.m., at which point you doze off and a baby (or two) *does* wake up. Now you're completely exhausted, irritated, and crying.

Which Symptoms Require Attention?

- Blues that don't go away after several weeks
- Stronger feelings of depression: feelings of hopelessness, feeling overwhelmed, feelings of guilt or doubt
- Change in appetite
- Chronic fatigue
- Recurrent thoughts of death/suicide
- Compulsiveness over babies' care
- Anxiety attacks
- Previous history of PPD (or of depression, postpartum or otherwise, in oneself or family members)

Many new moms of multiples experience more serious symptoms in addition to the common symptoms of the baby blues. By the six-month mark, many moms of multiples are convinced they have developed Chronic Fatigue Syndrome. Many have a change in appetite simply because they don't have as much time to eat as they used to, and therefore can no longer eat as much in one sitting.

But when these symptoms don't go away, and especially when they are coupled for even ten seconds with anxiety attacks, thoughts of suicide, thoughts of doing harm to the babies, or true feelings of hopelessness, it's time to contact a professional ***immediately***. The bottom line is that if you feel overwhelmed to the point where you dread the days as they begin, you need to call someone. Call your obstetrician, and don't be put off by comments about your feelings being normal. Use phrases such as, "I think I have postpartum depression," or "I'm having scary feelings." And dads, please pay attention. Mom may not be able to recognize what's happening, and it will be up to you to get help for her.

It's important to pay attention to whether you feel you can manage your feelings of doubt, guilt, or exhaustion. Clinical PPD keeps women from doing what they need to do everyday—it keeps them from being able to meet the basic needs of themselves and their babies.

Different women require different solutions. One woman may need in-home help one or two days per week. One woman may need to sit in silence for twenty minutes each evening. One woman may need cleaning help, cooking help, or carpool help for a few weeks. And one woman may need antidepressant medication. But any woman feeling sad day-in and day-out needs something other than a friend, family member, or doctor telling her it's normal and will go away.

PPD—as well as challenging periods when new moms are battling more than typical baby blues—*can* be treated. The feelings mothers experience are nothing to be ashamed of. Neither are the myriad medications commonly used to treat those feelings. Think of it this way: If you have a bacterial infection, you take an antibiotic. If you have a yeast infection, you use a prescription anti-fungal cream. If you have a cut, you apply a Band-Aid. There's nothing shameful about being strong enough to get what your body needs when it needs it. There's nothing shameful about loving yourself and your family enough to do whatever you need to do to function as a happy, albeit tired, Mama.

Preparing for the Postpartum Period

Establish a Support System on the Home Front

Being aware of the signs of PPD is a major first step in addressing it, should it occur. When you spend your days sleep-deprived, tending to stitches in a delicate area of your body, and figuring out how to make a turkey sandwich while holding a baby in each arm, it can be challenging to identify you middle name in a pinch, let alone identify if you are in need of additional assistance.

One of the best ways to take the "Is-how-I'm-acting-normal?" burden off yourself is to have a discussion—if at all possible, *before* the babies are born—with someone you both know well and completely trust. It's also important that this person is someone who sees you or talks to you with frequency so he or she can realistically identify a change in your attitude that goes beyond a "normal" response to childbirth and all that comes with it. If this person is a woman and has had a baby, that experience may provide an additional advantage because she will understand the emotions of a new mom, and will be able to provide strong support from that perspective.

Many women find their husband to be the best person to act in this capacity of "watchdog." There is often great trust in that relationship and strong knowledge of each other's personalities and ways of dealing with stressful situations. Another option is to enlist the help of a friend, mother, or mother-in-law. This person's job, at the end of the day, is to provide emotional support to you and to notify someone else—your husband first and foremost—should she become concerned that you need some extra short-term support of one variety or another.

In many cases, women report that simply having someone to talk to about their feelings and reassure them that they are not doing anything wrong and are not a bad mother is all they need. They problem solve together and find solutions. It's feeling all alone that often makes the situation seem unmanageable.

Establish a Multiples-Mom Support System

I've heard it time and time again: networking with other moms of multiples can make all the difference for new mothers of twins. While they love their friends with singletons, many new moms of twins long for the unique support that can only be provided by someone who's "been there, done that." Plus, moms with multiples who are operating on little sleep tend to quickly tire of hearing how difficult life is for their friend who is raising *just one baby*!

If you can attend a Marvelous Multiples or other multiple birth preparation class through your local hospital or community center, I encourage you to sign up as soon as you can. Strong friendships can be forged through these classes, and, other times, personalities that might only click due to the imminent arrival of multiples will be joined together. What you are looking for are relationships that will help all parties muddle through those first few hectic months. If any of the relationships goes beyond that—and many times they do— it's an added bonus.

If no such class is available in your area, many websites exist with chat rooms for expectant, new, and experienced moms of multiples. These chat areas can provide wonderful opportunities to post questions, seek advice, identify possible solutions, and network with other women going through a similar adventure.

I do advise women to beware of chat rooms where the chatter is predominantly negative. Many times, venting about how rough a time you're having is cathartic. But at the end of the venting session, you need a solution. Make sure you seek positive support, whether from a friend, family member, or the Internet.

Some doctors' offices have information on local resources for parents of multiples, and many cities have local chapters of mothers of twins clubs. Check out the website for the National Association of Mothers of Twins Clubs (http://www.namotc.org) to find a club in your area. Most are extremely open and welcoming to new members.

Accept Help

Always accept help when it's offered. Period. Anyone who offers help truly wants to do so. I've heard women express concern that people offering help possibly hoped it would not be accepted. In my mind, anyone who offers with the hope that you'll say "No," leaving him or her to protest, "Well, I offered," should have to do whatever they offered, plus some!

Don't be a martyr, I beg of you. Accept food, offers to rock babies, offers that allow you a nap, offers to pick up your groceries, *anything*. Remember Holly, the corporate superwoman who had a virtual boutique of baby equipment strategically spread throughout her kitchen and family room? When her girls were born approximately two months ahead of their due date, Holly's "I-can-do-anything" attitude kicked in immediately.

I remember an afternoon in the NICU (Jack and Henry were stationed right next to Holly's and Paul's triplets) when Holly was pumping breast milk to build a supply for the time when the girls could be bottle fed. I laughed because all I could hear was a loud sloshing sound (alongside the whirring of the breast pump), and suddenly Holly yelled, "Paul, switch!" She was overflowing the eight-ounce bottles she was pumping into and needed replacements.

I thought, as I struggled to get half an ounce using a breast pump, "Only Holly would be able to pump milk at this rate!" Within two weeks, her bags of frozen breast milk were overflowing from the hospital's freezer, and she'd almost filled her deep freezer at home.

Holly wanted to do it all on her own. But after a few weeks with the girls at home, she admitted that she needed help. She commented, "Even with poor postpartum memory, I remember every person who sent a meal or watched the kids so my husband and I could step out. Those memories are forever with me and I am so thankful for every one."

I tell anyone I know who is expecting twins that I clean a mean bathroom. While I won't do it for just anyone, I will do it for new moms of multiples. Sadly, no one has ever taken me up on it, and I know it's because they don't feel comfortable asking someone else to clean their bathroom. I understand that. But I would not offer if I weren't serious about it, so these women need to call my bluff and take that unpleasant task off of their to-do list! (I'm a bit nervous about how many people are now going to actually call my bluff, and send me an e-mail asking me to clean their bathroom! I'll tell you what: if you're local, I'll consider it.)

Nighttime Feeding Help
See the Reality of Sleep Deprivation section for detailed information on this topic.

Be Honest with Your Spouse
The first few months with your newborns is one of the most important periods to keep lines of communication open in your marriage—even if the verbal content isn't always pleasant. This is not the time to keep frustrations bottled up. The bottle will ultimately burst under the pressure, and the aftermath will not be pretty.

Make a promise to your spouse—again, before the babies are born, if possible—that you will do your best to be kind and tactful when you're having a tough day, hour, or moment. Ask him to do his best not to take you too seriously when you call him an idiot for not taking out the trash by 6:53 p.m. You are a team in this parenting experience, and it's extremely important to do the best you can to take care of each other—especially in the moments when one of you needs more care than the other.

Acknowledge that there will be times when your husband needs more care. I know this might sound absurd and, no, there shouldn't be more than, say, four of these occasions in the entire first year—ha, ha. However, while you're adjusting to your new role, your husband is also adjusting to his new role.

As often as I informed my husband that it wasn't possible for his feelings to be any more urgent, upsetting, or rational than mine, it would have been the right choice to, at least that same number of times, pretend I was grateful he had given up his monthly tee time to allow me to sleep in on Saturdays.

Don't Isolate Yourself

The first few months with multiples can be daunting if you want to get out of the house, but remember, you don't have to plan an eight-hour excursion to create a successful outing. You don't have to do a week's worth of grocery shopping or buy a season's worth of apparel. The key is to ensure that you aren't homebound for months on end. This can feel critically necessary when you have preemies to protect from germs during RSV season and/or it's the middle of winter and thirty below zero.

Some benign ways to get out that will do wonders for your sanity are: take a walk (weather permitting, of course), head to a friend's house for a quick visit, or take a drive. You might be surprised how much you can enjoy a simple car ride around town. The babies will hopefully sleep soundly, you can listen to the radio, and the fresh air will feel fantastic. You can even do this in pajamas and slippers!

If getting out with your babies is not an option early on for one reason or another, take the opportunity to get out by yourself or with a friend a couple of times a week.

Stand on the back porch and look at the stars, take a brief walk, go out for a quick coffee or dessert, or, again, drive around and listen to classical music (or any music that makes you feel good). The idea is to get a change of scenery and some fresh air while reminding yourself that you are indeed part of a larger world outside the four walls of your home.

Notes Nancy Bowers, RN, BSN, MPH, author of *The Multiple Pregnancy Sourcebook*, and founder of Marvelous Multiples (a very busy woman indeed), "One thing I always tell couples is to try to keep a normal day/night schedule, even if the babies were up all night and they have no idea what day (or night) it is. In the morning, open the blinds, put on the coffee, get dressed (if you can), and act like it's morning. Regular exposure to sunlight is important in maintaining your circadian rhythm, which helps keep biological processes functioning normally (including sleep patterns and hormones). It may even help the babies begin to adapt as well—awake in the daytime, and asleep at night!"

Be Patient

It's so important to be patient with yourself and your new family during this time of transition. Try not to have too many expectations of anyone as you're adjusting to so many changes in your life. The fact is, having one baby, or two babies, or seven babies changes your life in ways you can't possibly imagine. You can't imagine in how many wonderful, amazing ways your babies will enrich your life. And you can't imagine in advance the various challenges you may face and to what degree.

You have to take it all as it comes and be flexible and patient enough to glide from one moment to the next to avoid being so thrown so far by one that it's nearly impossible to see the next one coming. Make sure you're at the top of the list of people to care for during this postpartum phase, and it will help to ensure that your perspective is one of "I'm going to make it!"

THE REALITY OF SLEEP DEPRIVATION

People who say they sleep like a baby usually don't have one.
                                          —Leo J. Burke

How many times have you heard, "Enjoy your sleep now; you won't get much of it later." And how many times have you wondered, "How bad can sleep deprivation really be?"

I'll tell you two things. First, people who have children joke about sleep deprivation because they don't remember it well. They block the experience the same way women who give birth without anesthesia block the "discomfort" of childbirth; if they didn't, they'd have stopped after the first child. This selective amnesia is nature's way of ensuring survival of the species. Sleep deprivation is an experience every new parent goes through, and it is an experience every new parent survives. But it's nonetheless wise to be prepared for the reality of it.

In the first few weeks after twins arrive, most parents feel an extreme state of euphoria and have a high amount of adrenaline coursing through their systems. The euphoria won't necessarily dissipate. The adrenaline will.

Once you or your spouse needs to return to work, the sleep deprivation issue will become clearer. Your ability to catnap throughout the day—except for those times when the babies are miraculously sleeping at the same time for more than two minutes—won't be as great. Here's the thing: sleep deprivation is nasty. Not only does it make you cranky and clumsy and unable to see your eyelashes when applying mascara, it slows your physical recovery from childbirth. Your body needs restorative sleep to heal both physically and mentally.

In scientific studies, a prolonged lack of sleep (or, more specifically, a prolonged lack of quality sleep) has been shown to cause irritability, illness, and compromised performance. Certain stages of sleep are required in order for the brain, as well as certain other organs and muscles, to regenerate so they can function optimally. After extended periods without sleep, the brain's neurons actually begin to malfunction and a person's behavior is affected.

Keep in mind that sleep deprivation has been used as a form of torture for these very reasons. Its negative effects are well documented. While this all sounds ghastly, it also provides a logical explanation for your more frantic moments. Just think, you can end an argument by proclaiming, "Sorry honey, it's not me. The neurons in my brain are merely malfunctioning."

Now, supposedly, some of the affected organs and muscles can regenerate properly if a person merely rests. They key, however, is that she must be resting in a *quiet* environment. When you have newborn twins, if you have the opportunity to relax in a quiet environment, trust me, you will be unconscious within eleven seconds.

In other studies, it has been shown that sleep-deprived individuals have no functioning in the temporal lobe of the cerebral cortex, which is associated with the processing of language (so I suppose new parents can argue that they had no idea what they were saying when they told their spouse to move out!). Some other area of the brain, however, comes to the rescue of the temporal lobe. This explains why sleep-deprived individuals can actually still speak when they haven't slept for forty-eight hours. I still use the excuse that I can speak but have no idea what I'm actually saying when David and I get into an argument, and I know I'm being irrational.

One very large problem with sleep deprivation is that it has also been shown to cause difficulties in thinking creatively. New parents of twins need all the creativity they can muster—especially in the wee hours of the morning.

While the reality of sleep deprivation is almost sure to hit every household with a newborn or two in it, it will hopefully be short-lived and manageable with a bit of forethought. Management of such a state is a good idea not only because sleep deprivation does cause irritability, it weakens one's immune system. And the *last* thing you need with two newborns in the house is to get sick!

I'll be honest: David and I were idiots in this area (and I'm sure that—due to the lack of sleep—I let him know I thought he was an idiot on more than a few occasions). We didn't have family members living nearby to help on a regular basis, but in the initial weeks, when one side of our family was with us, we didn't ask for assistance with nighttime feedings. We simply didn't want to impose.

I'm too smart to suggest, the way everyone in your world has probably already suggested, that you nap when the twins nap. First of all, they will rarely nap simultaneously in the beginning. Second, if you have older children, you will be busy with them if and when the twins do nap simultaneously. The third, and probably biggest obstacle of all, is that I'd be willing to place bets that you are a Type A personality. Most mothers of multiples are for some reason. Therefore, even if you tell yourself you should nap when the babies nap, you won't. You'll be too obsessed with cleaning the kitchen, or folding the laundry, or finishing decorating the nursery, or plucking your eyebrows. Occasionally, you may doze off while the babies slumber. But you won't schedule it, and it will be a blessed miracle if and when it does occur.

In lieu of the above, then, I propose an alternate solution to managing sleep deprivation. When Jack and Henry were well over a year old, I learned of several local labor and delivery or NICU nurses who provided nighttime nursing assistance. Paid by the hour, some were available on an as-needed basis, while others required a contract that ensured they were paid for a certain number of hours per week whether they actually worked or not. Really, I almost lost my mind when I learned of these folks.

When you are paying someone to help you, there's no room to feel you're imposing. And when you're so tired that you truly need—possibly require—this level of assistance, you're also too tired to read the credit card statement or the checkbook balance and get bummed about the cost of it all.

If you get to a point where you're completely exhausted, consider asking a friend or family member for some nighttime help, or seeking out and hiring a professional. The cost may feel daunting, but it will only require a short-term shift in budgetary resources, and it will be *well* worth it.

I know women who hired a nurse on an as-needed basis after they fell asleep in the shower. I know women who believed strongly in hiring a nurse on an as-needed basis, and hired one for two or three nights in a row. One night with eight hours of uninterrupted sleep is heavenly, but if it's your first night in a while, it's likely your body (not used to such luxury) won't sleep soundly for those eight hours. Or it might sleep *very* soundly for eight hours. Either result is an indication that another night or two of such slumber is needed to get the full restorative effect of sleep and be ready to start fresh.

Women who hire a nurse requiring a contract, but who cannot afford or don't choose to hire her full-time, often hire her for every other night, or twice per week. This gives them a break when things are not consistently peaceful for eight hours straight, but aren't in such straights that they need two to three nights of consecutive assistance.

If you are interested in finding such a resource, check first with your local hospital. Many of the labor and delivery or NICU nurses offer nighttime nursing services on their days off. If you don't have luck with that approach, call other local hospitals or ask a local twins club for resources other multiples moms have heard of or used.

ANTICIPATING THE STORKS: THE FATHER'S SIDE
by Bob Evanosky

The biggest thing I remember is that there was just no transition. You hit the ground diapering.

—Paul Reiser

Listen up, guys! Here's the crash course on fathering twins in the first year.

When Elizabeth asked me to write this section, my first question was, "When?" I carved out time because the truth is, I have a great perspective from which to write. I have spent half of my sons' lives as the primary breadwinner and half as the primary caretaker. I have seen it from both sides and, frankly, while there are days when I'm not sure which angle is better, I would not trade any of it for even a second.

Let me start by saying: women are amazing. Most men simply could not endure what women go through to bring these babies into the world. When our boys were born on November 5 by Cesarean section, I looked down and saw my wife, Sonya's, uterus on her stomach. At that moment, I thought to myself, *"Geez,* they have her uterus on the outside of her body. This is wild!" Then, I thought, "Thank God she's the one with the uterus because you would *not* get me to do this!"

The biggest hurdle in this game of fathering multiples is the high learning curve—one you must master quickly and, often, on-the-fly. We must be thankful every second for the fact that women are ten times more prepared than men for this parenting thing, no matter how many babies they are expecting. They are naturally maternal. They educate themselves to the "nth" degree through the Internet, books, support groups, and other women.

The man's approach tends to be more of the "I'll-deal-with-it-as-it-comes" variety. We think, "It can't be *that* hard." Men are often more laid back about the details, the "how" and "when" of doing everything. Women feel they have the responsibility as mothers to get as much information as possible in order to be the best mothers they can be. In some ways, this discordance in approach is good because it allows one of you to be a little more laid back and relaxed. It can also cause big problems.

What may happen is that your wife feels you aren't interested in what is happening to her physically and emotionally during her pregnancy or in the ways your lives will change. Your wife may assume she'll take care of it all. That may make her feel overwhelmed. Or, she may feel you aren't as excited or happy as she is or that you don't really care.

If I were to do it again, I'd definitely be more supportive of Sonya by making certain I read the same books she read, and I would discuss them with her. Why is that important? Because *she* finds it of high value.

While you'd rather pick up the latest copy of *Sports Illustrated* or *In Fisherman*, opt instead for reading the stack of pregnancy, childbirth, and child-rearing books she's accumulated by her side of the bed. Do it in support of her. There were things I took for granted that I would have known had I read what Sonya read. Once our boys were born, my wife was frustrated that I didn't know these things. And 2:00 a.m. isn't a great time to ask a woman who's recently birthed twins why the babies aren't on a reliable schedule yet at ten days old! Reading with her would have made everything run much more smoothly.

Armin Brott's books on fatherhood are wonderful resources. He also has a new DVD available called *Toolbox for New Dads*. In about two hours of watching, it sums up much of what you need to know. There are several humorous books written by dads (clearly, men know what it takes to get us to read about parenting). If you need a book with comedic value to help you understand what the next years hold, check out *Keeping the Baby Alive till Your Wife Gets Home* by Walter

Roark, *Mack Daddy: Mastering Fatherhood without Losing Your Style, Your Cool, or Your Mind* by Larry Bleidner, or *The Guy's Guide to Surviving Pregnancy, Childbirth, and the First Year of Life* by Michael Crider. This is, of course, only a sampling of the books by and for expectant and new fathers. The fact is, many resources are now available to assist you in this transition, so there's no reason not to pick one up.

The Babies Are Here!

During the 0- to 3-month period, it's critical to remember that women are still recovering from the birth, and possibly from bed rest and a difficult pregnancy and/or delivery. Thus, the period of time from birth until the babies are three-months-old is the most intense period on a number of levels. Many twins spend some time initially in the NICU. The number of days the babies spend there can vary.

During this period, it's important to be honest about your feelings, both with yourself and with your wife. Use other parents, if you have them available to you (long-time friends, or perhaps new friends you might have met in a multiples class), for support. Utilize NICU doctors and nurses as well. Be prepared for the transitional issues your babies might face, such as the inability to regulate their body temperatures, undeveloped sucking reflexes, and feeding issues. Understand that transitional issues are often a "one step forward, two steps back" proposition. Ultimately, the babies will be fine, but you have to be patient.

Believe me, it's in your best interest to prepare for these issues up-front. In a way, I was lucky. Most of the babies from our multiples class were born a few weeks ahead of ours. I saw several of them in the NICU. Our babies didn't have some of the issues others had, so I felt okay about their condition. Had I not seen some of the other babies, I might not have been as strong. It's almost always a function of time for all the transitional prematurity issues to clear themselves up.

Once the babies are home, Phase Two begins. This phase is all about making it work, minute by minute. During this 0- to 3-month period, your wife is really going to need you. You don't always have a huge job in this process, but when you're called to the plate, you have to hit a grand slam, because that's when your wife badly needs you.

My biggest piece of advice: if you work outside the home, don't walk in the door at the end of the day and ask your wife what she did all day. For the first five months of our sons' lives, Sonya was the primary caregiver. As a pilot, I was often gone for three to four days at a time, and after walking in the front door, without saying it, I would think, "What went on here? This is chaos!" After those first five months, I retired from my job to be the primary caregiver, and Sonya went back to work.

After my first two weeks at home, I wanted to shoot myself. Ten days into it, I told myself, "I've made a huge mistake. What have I done? I just resigned from a major airline job that only 50,000 people in the world have, and I walked away from it for *this!*" But what I needed was a realignment of my expectations.

Believe me, a man who works nine hours a day or longer has unrealistic expectations of what really goes on at home while he's not there. I know because I've been on both sides. In those first two weeks as the primary caregiver, I had to become a woman.

What I couldn't handle, and what put me totally over the edge, was finding out that I had to arrange *my* entire schedule around the boys. I initially thought I'd be able to force them onto my schedule, but that just didn't work. It's fair to say that men can't understand this all-day-with-the-babies lifestyle having not experienced it. They must admit they can't understand it, yet at the same time appreciate that it's hard. Your wife doesn't get paid, but her job is one of the most important of all. And it never ends! You don't work as hard at any job as you do as the primary caregiver.

As the primary caregiver, my day is solid from 5:30 a.m. to 8:30 p.m. Few corporate jobs require that. There are some people who might work these hours of their own free will (and they are nuts), but this job requires it. You can't sit down when your kids need to eat. You can't put your kids to bed in pajamas with spit-up formula running down the front.

Men who are *not* the primary caregivers cannot assume their workday is over when they come home. They need to change clothes and dive in. Do some laundry, help feed the kids, send your wife out for a walk or a trip to the mall or bookstore—something to give her a break. Reassure her that what she's doing is invaluable. Understand what she needs to feel good and rejuvenated—perhaps going out alone at night for a few hours to run errands, going for a walk, or getting her hair cut. Many stay-at-home moms quickly begin to feel as though their lives are more or less one-dimensional.

There are so many ways you can help with this. After all, they say that having one child changes a woman's world—imagine two!

Finally, amidst the chaos and the awe, never forget the amazing, wonderful ways these new babies change your lives. For every smile you get with one baby, you get two with twins. In a matter of seconds, you add two more special little people to your family and to the world. These babies will depend on you for many years to come. So will your wife. If you step up to the plate with confidence and excitement, you will surely hit that grand slam!

TWO

0-3 Months: The Babies are Here!

MOST FREQUENT THOUGHTS DURING THIS PHASE

10. Are you sure I should wait only six weeks to have sex? Don't you mean six months?

9. I didn't know my body was capable of producing breasts this big.

8. Will these children ever stop eating? Is it even *possible* that they are having another growth spurt?

7. Will they ever sleep at the same time? Even for just fifteen minutes?

6. I cannot believe both of these babies were inside me at the same time.

5. While not exactly a fashion statement worthy of the cover of *Vogue*, a bag of frozen peas in my bra sounds great right about now.

4. How did I ever survive the days when we did not go out until 10:00 p.m.?

3. Whatever prompted me to *want* to stay up all night?

2. Why is it that immediately upon diapering this kid, he decides he's got to go...again?

1. How are parents with quads, quints, and more doing this?

If your babies have been born, let me start by saying how impressed I am that you've picked up a piece of reading material longer than a take-out menu! I think the first time I read something other than the local pizza delivery menu was when the boys were four months old, and I was tearing through *The Baby Whisperer* again in an attempt to make Tracy Hogg's approach work for twins.

WILL WE BE ALIVE IN THREE MONTHS?

You can turn painful situations around through laughter. If you can find humor in anything—even poverty—you can survive it.
                                                            —Bill Cosby

Yes, you will be alive in three months. The first few months are, in my opinion (and that of my girlfriends), the most challenging. More than anything, this is because you are recovering physically from pregnancy and childbirth while simultaneously adapting to the needs and personalities of your new babies.

Some new parents are adapting to and recovering from even more than this. Sheila, a mother of twin boys in Texas, welcomed her babies into the world at thirty-four weeks gestation. That, in and of itself, isn't terribly uncommon for a twin delivery. What *was* uncommon? The babies were delivered at home by her firefighter husband!

Sheila went to bed at 1:30 a.m. with no indication that she was going into labor. At 2:33 a.m. she awoke with stomach cramps and called her husband, who was on duty. She simply thought her stomach was upset. By 2:50 a.m., she knew she had more of a problem than an upset stomach, and called her husband again, to tell him to come home immediately.

"He walked in the door at 3:15 a.m., and according to the time on the 911 call, our first baby was born at 3:18 a.m. Our second son was born at 3:33 a.m.—in a breech position. The paramedics didn't arrive at our house until fifteen minutes after that." Both babies are happy and healthy today, and what a story their parents have to share with them when they get older!

To be perfectly honest, each phase (0-3 months, 3-6 months, and 6-12 months) is not necessarily any easier or harder than another, it's just different. Actually, that's not completely true. It *will* get easier. My mom summed it up well by saying, "It's not a different ballgame, just a different inning." And that's a good thing. The longer you play the same game, the more skilled you get, the more shortcuts you develop, and the better you play.

What makes it all work during this phase? Many things. Mostly the repetition of several key phrases. Do whatever it takes to keep these thoughts running through your head. Post them above the changing table (if you have one), on the front of your feeding logs, on the front of the refrigerator, and/or on your bathroom mirror (I realize you might not look into it that often).

Mantras for Keeping Your Sanity

- I will sleep again.
- I will keep my sense of humor.
- I will be flexible.
- Nothing magical happens at the six-week mark. (Don't let this comment discourage you. The knowledge that the six-week milestone isn't as magical as you might have been led to believe will help. One day you'll wake up, realize a hurdle has been crossed, and that another awaits. At least you will no longer be dealing with the first one. When our babies were about four months old, I found myself saying with great frequency, "Crawl in different directions, crawl up the walls for all I care, JUST SLEEP!")
- It matters not if I shower each day or put on clothes. After all, I've been dreaming of a day I could spend in pajamas from dawn until, well, the next dawn.
- We would not have been given these babies if we could not do this.
- Breathe. Smile. Love.
- Sweet Jesus, if you're there, *help!*

This chapter is titled, "0-3 Months: Ready...Set...Feed!" because feeding is what this time period is all about. You wouldn't believe how much of these three months are focused, directly or indirectly, on eating. First, there's the babies' need to eat (a lot and often). Then, there's your need to eat. Then, there's the amount of analysis you will do around how much (and how often) your babies are eating, and how that relates to the fact that they aren't sleeping.

You'll analyze and analyze again, modify feeding schedules, find all kinds of ways to eat food yourself while juggling one or two babies, learn how much good food can be eaten with one hand, and then go back to another analysis of your babies' eating patterns, their sleeping patterns related to their eating patterns, and their eating patterns related to gas, constipation, and other common newborn challenges. Like I said, this phase revolves mostly around eating.

But know that these three months are also going to be a lot of fun. Be good to yourself, and focus on the "lot of fun" part. If approached the right way, this time will provide you with much laughter. Many opportunities exist for bonding with your spouse, and you'll gain a new regard for the pleasures of sleeping more than an hour at a time, eating a full meal while it's still warm, showering more often than once every three days, and finding time to put on real clothes before the sun goes down each day. Plus, you'll develop a *huge* regard for clothes unstained by spit-up!

This period will also give you unmatchable blessings: the newly formed bonds with your children, the feeling of a heart ready to explode when you see those first smiles, the memory of a first "conversation," love for the smell of a freshly bathed baby, and the joy of seeing your husband develop amazing relationships with each baby, just to name a few.

FEED!

There are times when parenthood seems nothing but feeding the mouth that bites you.

—Peter De Vries

As I'm sure you are aware, there are two ways to feed your beautiful babies: breast and/or bottle. The approach you decide upon is personal to you and your spouse, but the one you use is the right one for you at the time. Be comfortable with it and confident in it. Do your best with the decision you make; that is all you can ask of yourself.

Nearly everyone around you will have an opinion.

Regardless of what the rest of the world might say about it, however, other mothers of multiples will respect your decision to do either or both with no questions asked. Go with your gut, and know that the "multiples" sorority, at a minimum, supports you 100 percent no matter your decision.

BREASTFEEDING TWINS: CAN IT BE DONE?

A pair of substantial mammary glands have the advantage over the two hemispheres of the most learned professor's brain in the art of compounding a nutritive fluid for infants.
                              —Chief Justice Oliver Wendell Holmes

Yes! I know several women who successfully breastfed their twins until they were a year old. I know of several women who exclusively breastfed their twins with a toddler in the house.

Breastfeeding provides physical and psychological benefits to both mother and baby. Studies have shown that breastfeeding is an effective preventive mechanism for many childhood illnesses, including ear infections, upper and lower respiratory infections, sudden infant death syndrome (SIDS), and allergies, to name a few. Reduced rates of breast and ovarian cancer have also been shown among women who breastfed.

Further, when asked how they lost their pregnancy weight so quickly, many new moms respond, "Breastfeeding!" Breastfeeding causes your uterus to contract more frequently and your body to burn excess calories. Now, breastfeeding never provided me with the same weight-loss benefits it provided Chrissy, whose story is profiled below. I breastfed my daughter, and remember thinking at the end of the first three months, "These calories are going straight from my breasts to my rear end" (but I am usually the exception on a lot of things).

I remember the night my husband and I sat in the second of five Marvelous Multiples birthing classes at our local hospital. While the lactation consultant talked to the group about breastfeeding multiples, everyone's eyes fixated on her. Some were genuinely intent on breastfeeding their babies, and others were more interested in how she would explain with a straight face how to breastfeed two at once.

Each woman was given two baby dolls. This was the first time most of us had a true sense of what it would be like to be in charge of two babies at once. After all, we had all held the baby of a friend or relative, and in my case, I had a daughter at home. But two babies at once was an entirely different proposition. Imagine how our new friends Paul and Holly a few seats away felt; they were going to be juggling three!

The consultant demonstrated several techniques for breastfeeding two babies simultaneously. It was at that moment that reality began to set in. Many expectant parents remained determined, and I heard some giggles as well as comments like, "Okay, this isn't *too* bad," going around the room.

Honestly, it wasn't the "how" of breastfeeding two babies at once that had people's jaws on the floor, it was the "how often." I will never forget the look on Mollie's face as the lactation consultant explained how often we could expect our children to eat each day in the beginning. Eight to twelve times per day. Per baby. That's right, folks, you've done your math correctly. I could see Mollie doing the math with her eyes.

That's a possible total of twenty-four feedings per day. Now, how many hours are there in a day again? Oh yes, twenty-four. And each feeding can take, say, thirty minutes including a diaper change (or two) if you're feeding babies individually. That leaves about one minute per hour to use the bathroom, eat, get dressed, shower, do dishes, make formula, tend to the two-year-old, and complete whatever other miscellaneous chores need to be done.

At that point I'm fairly sure I started laughing, but I swear, I thought Mollie was going to burst into tears.

The first decision you must make is if *you* want to breastfeed your babies. New moms often feel pressure to breastfeed from their own mothers or their mothers-in-law, husbands, or society in general. This pressure not only can make the process more difficult, it can make the new mom feel horribly guilty if she experiences challenges.

Should you choose to breastfeed, there are products that will assist you with your efforts, and I will detail each below. There are three things, however, you should arm yourself with immediately. Without these three, your breastfeeding experience will not go smoothly no matter what other supplies you have. They are: support, support, and support. The stories that follow of women who've successfully breastfed their twins will affirm this fact. Even with an arsenal of breast pumps, breast pads, bottled water, and frozen peas, you will, at some point, require an adequate amount of support from your spouse, a friend, and/or a lactation consultant to get your babies established as breastfeeders.

Of course, there are circumstances where breastfeeding any number of babies is not possible no matter how much support you might have. If one or both babies is, for some reason, unable to latch on; if there is a weight-gain concern with a baby that prompts your baby's doctor to recommend supplementation or sole feeding with formula; if a baby has a milk protein allergy that a mom can't accommodate through customizing her diet without having to subsist on air; if a woman's nipples are shaped in a way that makes latching on extremely difficult; or if a new mom is simply so exhausted and frustrated that she believes she might lose her mind if she has to continue attempting to breastfeed, it's a perfectly logical and rational solution to move to Plan B (Plan B being bottle-feeding).

I find it a cruel act of nature that the three or four hardest weeks when you will have to establish breastfeeding are those directly following the babies' birth. You're physically recovering from childbirth; trying to figure out the whole "parenting" thing; exhausted; dealing with sore nipples, clogged ducts, and engorgement; unsure whether the babies are getting enough to eat; unsure whether the babies' crying is related to something you ate and, if so, what; concerned that if you can't figure out what food they are reacting to, you will have to eliminate everything from your diet and, therefore, starve yourself; possibly dealing with outside pressure to breastfeed even though you aren't sure that's what you want to do; and on and on.

Many women who have successfully breastfed twins contend that once you make it through the first three to four weeks, you're home free. I was not able to breastfeed Jack or Henry past the four-week mark, but I concur that the three- to four-week intro to this sport is the most critical. How do I know? Because I successfully and exclusively breastfeed Grace for three months and Baby Number Four for ten months. (Yes, there was a fourth baby. More on that in *Ready or Not...There We Go! The REAL Experts' Guide to the Toddler Years with Twins*).

By the four-week mark, most babies have learned how to latch on, moms have learned which positions work best, and mom's breasts are becoming accustomed to nursing and are, therefore, less sore. As the babies get bigger you'll get better at positioning them so they can breastfeed simultaneously, and you'll feel better physically with each passing day. Many of the initial barriers will abate. But those first three to four weeks can feel like an eternity when you're trying to juggle all those issues and the emotions that come with new motherhood at the same time.

Before we get too far down the road into the actual breastfeeding, let's step back and discuss those three critical components I mentioned earlier. If you are determined to have a successful breastfeeding experience, it's imperative that you receive positive support from the get-go.

If you decide to give breastfeeding a try, I hope, at a minimum, that your husband is on board. I don't think I've ever heard of a husband who was *not* supportive of his wife's desire to breastfeed. One, it's healthy for both mom and babies. Two, it's free. Three, it means he is somewhat excused from nighttime feedings (take note of the word "somewhat"). And four, your breasts will be larger than life, which is sure to thrill him. But be sure that he's more than just supportive at heart. He also needs to be supportive in action.

Explain to your husband that breastfeeding can be challenging at first. You'll need him to encourage you, to praise your efforts, to bring you a warm heating pad if you get a blocked duct, to bring you something to drink while you are nursing, and to be the person who doesn't let you give up when you mention that you might, at 3:00 a.m.

It's somewhat the same situation as it is when a woman decides on a natural childbirth. She needs someone with her who knows that she can make it through and who won't let her fall back on the epidural when the going gets really rough. At the same time, she needs someone who knows her and her limits and knows when the going *has* gotten too rough.

Fortunately, I know many women whose husbands are unbelievably supportive as their wives begin breastfeeding. They follow her lead and offer encouragement, but are more than happy to go to Plan B if that's what's best for their wife—not because they aren't disappointed, but because they love their wife, and want to support her unconditionally.

I also know several moms of twins whose mothers and mothers-in-law have been incredibly supportive. Not pushy, simply supportive. It's amazing the positive effect of just telling a woman who's attempting to breastfeed, "Good job!"

Let's start at the beginning. Your babies may or may not be able to breastfeed in the hospital. The babies may be in your recovery room with you and begin nursing right away.

They may be in the NICU unable to nurse, and you might need to pump your breast milk and take it to the nurses in the NICU to feed or store for your babies. Finally, your babies may attempt nursing with various lactation aids, if for no other reason, to begin the bonding process. Every situation is different, and lactation consultants are trained to help you through your own.

In the hospital as well as after returning home, many new moms focus on nursing their babies and then following up with supplemental formula if necessary. Some women have someone else feed the babies breast milk and/or formula from a bottle while they pump nearby to encourage their supply until the babies are stronger and able to latch on. Some women pump just after and/or between feedings to build their supply and create a stock of breast milk for the freezer.

It's important that the nurses assigned to your babies in the hospital, the lactation consultant, and your pediatrician once you are discharged, are supportive of your desire to breastfeed. It's unlikely, but should you be paired with a lactation consultant or a NICU nurse who tries to talk you out of breastfeeding for purely logistical reasons, request another nurse or consultant.

One day, a NICU nurse who had older twins was caring for Jack and Henry, and because her breastfeeding experience was not positive, she was not terribly supportive of my desire to nurse our babies. After a challenging session, she commented, "You know, it's okay to feed them formula" (which I was already doing on a supplemental basis).

At that point, I was too tired and sore to hear what people were saying to me on any level, and not having anyone enthusiastically encouraging me to breastfeed, I felt strongly that our babies would not be sustained long-term on breast milk alone. Being encouraged to bottle-feed instead of remaining optimistic and positive about the fact that I *could* breastfeed definitely didn't help.

During this time, the nurses may need to supplement or feed solely with formula—possibly a fortified formula designed to meet the babies' unique needs. Be sure to request a consultation with a lactation consultant if this is your situation. She can get you set up with a hospital-grade breast pump to express your breast milk and establish your milk supply, and she can answer any questions you may have.

In many cases, your babies can be fed the colostrum and subsequent breast milk you express. Even if they get only three drops of colostrum followed by an ounce of formula, those three drops will benefit them. Your body knows exactly at what point in gestation your babies were born, and it produces colostrum based on the specific nutritional needs of your babies based on their birth date. So, whether it's a drop or an entire feeding of colostrum or breast milk, it's beneficial.

Once your babies are attempting to latch on, ask the nurses or lactation consultants to help you figure out what position or positions work best and which positions you can use to nurse both babies at once. Be prepared for the fact that nursing both babies at once may not work in the beginning. Your babies are learning to breastfeed just as you are learning. You may need to have one-on-one nursing time with each baby for a few weeks until breastfeeding is well established.

In addition, the babies are usually small enough in the beginning that it may be difficult to single-handedly arrange them into position and have them latch on. Having a helper can be critical. Once you get one baby positioned and latched on, another adult can position the second baby (and be on standby should one baby need help getting latched on again).

Should you determine that you want to breastfeed in whole or in part, go for it! There are many resources available to assist you. Take advantage of them as often as necessary.

As a side note, many breastfeeding mothers wonder if their breasts will ever return to a normal size. Much to your husband's dismay, I'm sure, the answer is yes. Might I add that not only will they return to a normal size, they will regress to the size they were just after you hit puberty.

Chrissy's story

Before our twin girls were born, I decided that I wanted to breastfeed. I found value in the long-term benefits of breastfeeding, both for myself and for the girls. And the cost of breastfeeding, well, you can't beat that! I set an initial goal to breastfeed them for six months.

Our girls were born five and a half weeks early. When they were in the NICU, their feedings were supplemented with formula because my body wasn't yet producing enough milk to keep them well nourished. I didn't have any feelings of "failure" at not being able to provide enough breast milk. At that point, everything about having twins was still so new to me. One of my strongest memories of that time was feeling I needed to do my best to increase my milk supply as much as possible and set up a routine for doing so.

Having the girls in the NICU was a blessing in disguise. It allowed me time to heal from my C-section and work on my milk supply. The biggest issue in the beginning was the fact that my supply took some time to become fully established.

I pumped every two to three hours around the clock, both at the hospital and at home. Using a hospital-grade breast pump was extremely important. Once the girls no longer needed feeding tubes, I put each girl to the breast at each feeding when I was in the NICU, unless it tired her out. The more skin-to-skin contact I had with each baby, the faster my milk supply became established.

Before long, I was thrilled to be bringing cups of breast milk to the NICU instead of just small tubes! The NICU nurses always did a wonderful job of making sure to feed the babies my pumped breast milk before giving them formula.

We brought the girls home when they were a week and a half old. My mother-in-law stayed with us for the first two weeks, and my mom stayed the next three weeks. My mother-in-law strongly believes in breastfeeding, and she provided lots of support.

I knew that remaining hydrated would play a huge part in not only getting my milk supply established but keeping it established long-term, so I kept glasses of water all over the house. I drank before I pumped—suggested to me by another mom—to get more milk out of that particular pumping session.

The first two weeks at home, I needed help getting the babies properly positioned. I nursed them one at a time. I nursed a baby on one side and then pumped the other side directly afterward. This way, I didn't have to juggle two babies per feeding while both they and I were learning how to breastfeed. Then, for the next feeding, I nursed the other baby, and someone bottle-fed pumped breast milk to the baby who had nursed at the previous feeding. This approach enabled the babies to get comfortable with feedings from either breast or bottle.

Introducing a bottle early on worked well for us. If someone else had to feed them, they accepted a bottle. There was a time when they would only accept a bottle from my husband. It was almost impossible for me to bottle feed them because they smelled me and wanted to nurse instead. This may have been our girls' unique personalities, however, and not a hard and fast rule.

During our first two weeks at home, I worried that the girls weren't getting enough to eat because I could only pump an ounce or two per feeding. Our pediatrician's office had a lactation consultant on staff, and we weighed each baby in the office right before and right after a feeding to see exactly how much she got. They got more from me than I was able to pump! I learned that the amount of breast milk a woman can pump does not necessarily indicate how much she's producing when her babies are actively nursing. My girls were more efficient at nursing than I thought.

Having a lactation consultant at our pediatrician's office providing strong support and encouraging me to bring the babies to the office to weigh them anytime I was concerned was wonderful.

Numerous times, however, I wanted to stop breastfeeding. Many days I felt more like a cow than a mother. I took it day by day, and to this day I cannot believe how quickly that first year flew by. When I experienced a breastfeeding challenge in those early weeks, the support I received from family and our pediatrician's office was extremely beneficial. Plus, reminding myself of the health benefits both to myself and to the babies, coupled with the constant acknowledgment of how much money we were saving, provided sufficient motivation for me to push through that particular challenge. Seeing how big the girls were getting, and knowing that that growth came from my breast milk, was very rewarding.

After two weeks or so at home, the girls were quickly latching on, and I started nursing them simultaneously. Learning to nurse them simultaneously was one of my most successful strategies because I had two satisfied babies at the same time and on the same schedule. I held each of them in the football hold with the Boppy Pillow in front and a pillow behind my back for support. At one point, I was nursing both girls at once and talking to someone on the phone using my headset attachment!

Once I reached my initial goal of breastfeeding the girls for six months, the process was so easy and we had such a good routine going that it didn't make sense to stop. Plus, once the girls were eating solid foods, they needed to nurse less often. The breastfeeding got easier and easier, and actually became more enjoyable for me.

I continued to take prenatal vitamins while I was breastfeeding, and I wore nursing bras that did not have an underwire and were easy to get off and on. Bras with flaps that snap are far easier than those with hooks!

I nursed my girls exclusively for their entire first year of life. It is work in the beginning for sure, but it's doable. I encourage all new moms of twins who wish to breastfeed their babies to use the resources available to them, and not give up!

As I mentioned earlier, I also know women who exclusively nursed their babies even with a toddler at home. The experience of a woman who successfully breastfed her twins with not one older child at home, but two, follows.

Lora's Story

I have always been a strong believer in breastfeeding. I nursed my older children, Vanessa and Brandon, and when our twins, Tyler and Nick, were born, I was determined to breastfeed them as well.

First, some background on my breastfeeding history. I nursed Vanessa (who was six years old when the twins were born) until she was fifteen months old. When Vanessa was four months old, I returned to work. We had never introduced a bottle, formula, or a pacifier, and by the four-month mark she would not accept any milk except breast milk—and she insisted on receiving it directly from me. It was a nightmare. I pumped, but she would not drink the milk, not even from a medicine dropper. I breastfed her in the morning before leaving for work. My parents watched her during the day, and they lived close to my workplace. My dad picked me up each day at lunch, and I went to their house to nurse her and eat lunch. I then returned to work and nursed her again around four o'clock when I returned home. She began to cluster feed when she knew I was there, and was able to meet her nutritional needs.

A few years later, I learned that I was pregnant again. After the experience with Vanessa, I wanted our new baby, Brandon, to have at least one bottle of formula per day. The pressure I felt because of Vanessa's dependence on me scared me. No one else had the opportunity to feed her. Even my husband was unable to participate.

After his birth, Brandon received a bottle at the hospital each night. He never had any problem with "nipple confusion." Babies are smart. Mommy's milk requires more work to obtain, but it's also much sweeter than formula. Brandon learned that when he was nursing he needed to suck one way, and when he was being fed from a bottle he needed to suck a different way. The first few times he was bottle fed, I waited in the other room so he couldn't smell me.

When Brandon was nineteen months old, I learned I was pregnant with the twins. My obstetrician said, "Go home and wean your son—today. You can't nourish the babies inside you and yourself if you are breastfeeding." I followed his instructions and gradually weaned my son.

When the twins were born, I knew I wanted to nurse them. I knew it might be challenging, but I was determined. At the same time, I told myself that if breastfeeding didn't work, it was okay. I had a C-section, and I was sorer than I'd been after Vanessa's and Brandon's deliveries. I was blessed that our twins didn't have to spend time in the NICU. They were born three weeks early, but weighed nearly six pounds each.

The challenge when the babies are in your recovery room with you is getting positioned. I was sore, bleeding, and wary of my stitches! Scooping them out of their bassinets and getting both yourself and them positioned isn't easy if you don't have help.

A lactation consultant wasn't on duty after I delivered the twins. My initial plan was to nurse them individually and have one twin get a bottle of pumped breast milk. This proved nearly impossible because they were always hungry, and there was simply no time in between feedings to pump. I was nursing constantly. I soon changed course and decided to simply nurse them on demand and work on a more formal feeding and pumping schedule later on.

Unfortunately, with no lactation consultant on duty, the nurses at the hospital weren't terribly helpful. They were often not available to help me get the babies latched on, and often asked, "Why don't you just give them bottles? It's far easier." Their attitude made it quite tempting for me to give up. I was tired, sore, my hormones were completely unbalanced, and I felt like I was muddling through by myself.

As with Brandon, at night I sent the babies to the nursery to be fed a bottle of formula. This way, they got used to both bottle and breast. Once the babies and I came home from the hospital, my approach changed because I was immediately less confident. All of a sudden, I had four children to care for and no nursing staff to help me get a baby latched on or hold them while I unhitched my nursing bra. I had a toddler who needed me, a daughter who was adjusting to two more brothers and less time with me, and a phone ringing off the hook with folks who wanted to visit.

My husband was very supportive and helped me in any way he could. He knew how much I wanted to breastfeed, but always made sure I didn't feel like a failure during the rough patches. He reminded me that we had formula in the house, and it would all be okay.

I decided to state to everyone on the end of the endlessly ringing phone line that, unfortunately, I wasn't up for visitors yet. I simply wasn't comfortable sitting half-naked on the couch trying to nurse with an audience! I know people were disappointed to have to wait to see the babies, but I had to put my immediate family first.

I encouraged my older children to be involved in the breastfeeding experience with me, so they didn't see it as a time when they were left out. Vanessa read to me or to the babies while I nursed. We occasionally played games like Memory or Candyland. Brandon sat next to me, and I read him a picture book or he watched a video and we talked about the different things he saw. I told Vanessa and Brandon stories of how I'd nursed them and funny things they'd done while nursing. Vanessa, especially, loved this time hearing funny stories about herself.

My parents, in-laws, and my good friend, Renee, provided significant support to me. My dad even took a trip to Manhattan to buy me the EZ-2-Nurse twins nursing pillow— the foam version, not the inflatable one. He knew I didn't want to wait for it to ship! My mother and mother-in-law tag teamed for the first two weeks. One burped one baby so I could begin nursing the second one right away. They folded laundry, made sure I had enough to drink, and made me nutritious snacks. They also fed and entertained Vanessa and Brandon. Knowing that my older kids were happy and taken care of helped tremendously.

A feeding/diaper log was very important. I nursed each baby on only one side. My supply built to the point that each baby got what he needed from "his" side. But there were days when I'd grab a baby and wonder, "Who is this? And what side does he go on?" The feeding log helped us track who ate when and how many wet/dirty diapers they had, which in turn gave us confidence that they were getting enough to eat.

My supply was often highest in the morning and lowest in the evening, so in the evenings I often fed them more often than I did throughout the day.

Each time I wanted to quit, my friend reminded me how determined I was. She said if anyone could do it, I could. I truly don't believe I would have been able to nurse without the support of my family and friends. However, that need for support isn't exclusive to trying to nurse twins. It's necessary for any nursing experience.

I had a wonderful lactation consultant when I was nursing Brandon. Because the twins were born shortly after Brandon, I was able to call upon my memory of the strategies I learned from her. I e-mailed her on occasion for tips, and I knew she was only a phone call away if I needed more direct communication with her. One of her most important pieces of advice was to remember to breathe as the babies first started nursing. It helped with the discomfort and allowed my milk to let down more easily. She was not opposed to supplementing with formula and believed that any breast milk was better than no breast milk. Therefore, I didn't experience any guilt over giving them some formula.

I thought that when I went back to work I wouldn't be able to continue nursing because I didn't know when I'd have time to pump. I held a job-sharing teaching position. The twins were born in July, and I went back to work part-time in September. After asking for places in the office where I could pump, my co-workers were completely supportive, even altering their schedules on occasion so I could get my pumping sessions completed. I occasionally pumped in the car and even in the principal's office. The principal insisted it was the most exciting and important meeting that ever took place in her office!

At thirteen months, Tyler weaned himself. After three weeks, Nick realized Tyler was drinking milk from a sippy up, and clearly thought, "We're done with this? Okay!" He was then on to bigger and better things as well.

The bottom line is that nursing takes work, patience, and perseverance. But if your heart is in it, there is no obstacle you cannot overcome. There is a solution to every problem. There are dozens of products available to assist you, and you must take it a day at a time. Many times I'd say to my husband, "I cannot do this," and he'd counter with, "Lora, you *are* doing it!" And so I was.

Breastfeeding Essentials

Support
    I've discussed the need for support almost to death. I'll keep it at the top of the list, however, so you remember how important it is.

Soothies Gel Packs
    Soothies are a remarkable product designed to soothe

irritated nipples in the first few weeks of breastfeeding. They are stored in the refrigerator, and when you finish nursing, you put them between your nipples and your bra. They feel absolutely wonderful.

When I breastfed our daughter, and I used more of the Lamaze breathing techniques to get through the first five minutes of a breastfeeding session than I had during labor! But the discomfort you will experience in the early days and weeks of breastfeeding will subside. As long as your babies are positioned correctly, your nipples will become accustomed to nursing. From that point on, beyond the sensation of your milk letting down (a sensation, I swear, you will *never* forget), there won't be any strange or painful feeling associated with nursing whatsoever.

Lily Padz

For every woman sick and tired of leaking milk no matter how many breast pads she's wearing, Lily Padz are the solution. In fact, Lily Padz can be worn without a bra, so when you've had it with wearing a bra to bed, opt instead to stick on the Lily Padz between feedings. I didn't believe for a second that this product—or any product short of a rubber bra—would keep milk from leaking through my clothing, especially at night. Lily Padz proved me wrong.

High-Quality Breast Pump

When getting your supply established is critical, the best breast pump to use is a hospital-grade pump because it provides maximum effectiveness and efficiency. A baby sucks approximately forty to sixty times per minute. A hospital-grade breast pump cycles automatically about fifty times per minute, so it most closely resembles a baby's actual nursing pattern. This helps your let-down reflex occur in the same way it would if you were actually breastfeeding, and you are able to pump more milk in a shorter period of time. Hospital-grade pumps are also often more comfortable to use than their store-bought counterparts.

Many hospitals and lactation consultant groups have pumps you can rent from them, and they are well worth the rental cost. Don't neglect to check with your insurance company to see if they will cover any or all of the cost of renting a hospital-grade pump.

Lanolin

In the early days and weeks of breastfeeding, many moms need as many nipple-soothing products as they can get their hands on. Lanolin is a topical cream applied around the areola. It soothes the area and prevents it from becoming cracked (or helps heal it once it's already cracked). Applying Lanolin and Soothies Gel Packs after a nursing session go a long way toward soothing your nipples and preventing more damage.

Heating Pad with Moisture

Should you get a blocked duct, or have general breast tenderness in the initial weeks, a heating pad with steam works wonderfully. This type of heating pad comes with a little pack that you wet and stick inside the heating pad cover. As the pad heats up, the wet pack provides warm moisture and soothes the affected area. A warm washcloth works equally well, but it quickly gets cold. When you need to unclog a blocked duct, try using a warm compress for fifteen to twenty minutes.

Put the heating pad on the part of your breast with either a blocked duct or where it's sore, and gently massage as though you are trying to work the block toward your nipple. Lamaze breathing techniques, or any deep breathing technique, will come in handy while you are doing this.

High-Quality Nursing Bra

High quality nursing bras aren't any less expensive than high-quality everyday bras. Since they will typically be used for a year or less, many women cut corners by purchasing inexpensive nursing bras.

Inexpensive isn't necessarily bad, but cheap is. If you choose a bra with flaps that come down when you nurse, opt for flaps that snap to the straps, not hook. Another option is to buy nursing bras that look like athletic bras. I always liked these because, when it was time to nurse, I just pushed everything—shirt and bra together—up. It's easier to get up and down, which is nice if you are nursing in public at any point. In addition, this style of bra is not binding, so it's not likely to cause the irritation an underwire bra might.

Helpful Nursing Pillow

Having proper support for the babies while you're nursing helps ensure that your back and neck don't take any more abuse than they have to from bending down to your babies.

Two supports I've consistently heard work well for nursing mothers of twins are the Boppy Pillow or the EZ-2-Nurse Foam Twin Nursing Pillow.

Strategies for Breastfeeding Babies Simultaneously

There are a multitude of positions you can use to breastfeed your babies simultaneously.

The Football Hold

Place a pillow on either side of your hips, or use a larger nursing pillow such as the Easy-2-Nurse twins nursing pillow. Place a baby on either side of you, on his side, with his feet pointing toward your back (holding the baby as you would a football as you run down the field). Cradle a baby's head in each of your hands. Use extra pillows if necessary to support the babies' heads at breast level and/or support your own back if the chair or couch you're sitting on is deep.

The Football/Cradle Hold

Again, use a pillow of some sort to hold the babies at breast level. Place one baby in the football hold and the other in the cradle hold.

The cradle hold is the most traditional breastfeeding position. The baby is cradled across your front, on a pillow for support, with his stomach and chest touching your body (if the baby's stomach is pointing toward the ceiling, you're not positioned properly). The baby's head is cradled in the crook of your arm (his ear, not the back of his head, should be resting on your arm).

Place the second baby in the football hold in your opposing arm. The head of the baby in the football hold should gently rest against the abdomen of the baby in the cradle hold.

I tried this position when Jack and Henry were in the NICU. Jack decided he was finished long before Henry; there was no one around, I was behind this whopping-big curtain, and I wanted to scream, "Um...could I get a little help here?" Had a nurse not come to check on me, I would still have one baby on my left breast and the other cradled in my right arm today.

The Cradle Hold

Place both babies in the cradle hold (baby's chest against your chest), with their bodies crossing each other's. This position typically works well with a large, firm nursing pillow across your lap or two bed pillows on top of one another.

Breastfeeding Resources

La Leche League International
An international resource for women committed to breastfeeding their children.
(847) 519-7730
http://www.lalecheleague.org

Nursing Mothers Advisory Council
A non-profit, volunteer organization serving specific counties in Pennsylvania and staffed by a group of women who have breastfed their children, the council is anxious to help others have a positive nursing experience. If you live outside Pennsylvania, utilize the site's Help section or send an e-mail to the group to request further assistance.
(215) 572-8044
http://www.nursingmoms.net

Another Woman Who Has Breastfed Twins
   As with every aspect of raising twins, the best source of support for breastfeeding is another mom who's been through it. Try to locate a mom of multiples through your prenatal class, local twins club, or online resource who has had a positive experience breastfeeding her twins. These women are usually all too willing to share their experience and provide suggestions and support, because it was that exact type of support that enabled them to be successful.
   Sheri Bayles, a nurse, internationally recognized and award winning Certified Lamaze Instructor, and International Board Certified Lactation Consultant (who also happens to have twin boys she breastfed for nine months) has an information-packed website. Be sure to visit this site at http://www.breastfeedingclass.com.
   Sheri offers a breastfeeding class on DVD for sale, answers many common breastfeeding questions, and offers a free e-mail newsletter for breastfeeding moms. Featured on NBC's *Today Show* and CBS's *Parent2Parent* as having taught over 4,000 couples (including some celebrities) to breastfeed their babies, she's a recognized leader in the field.
   Another strong advocate of breastfeeding multiples is Karen Kerkhoff Gromada. Karen works as a lactation consultant in Cincinnati, Ohio, has been a La Leche League instructor since 1977, and is the author or co-author of several books on raising and breastfeeding multiples.

Gromada's website provides a slew of links to sites such as online discussion groups for those wishing or attempting to breastfeed their multiples as well as links to various multiple pregnancy and birth sites. It's a great resource; be sure to see all that it has to offer at http://www.karengromada.com.

Local Support

If you're not sure, check to see if the hospital where you delivered your babies has lactation specialists on staff. If you worked with one while you were there, don't hesitate to call her for assistance, as they are always willing to help. Some cities also have independent lactation groups who offer guidance, supplies, and support. Check your yellow pages or ask your local hospital to see if one exists in your area.

BOTTLE-FEEDING

There ain't no such thing as wrong food.
> —Sean Stewart, *Perfect Circle*

I've received a few e-mails from women looking for support and advice because their husbands forbid them from feeding formula to their babies. These moms are completely and utterly exhausted—and not getting much assistance from their husbands in the way of moral or physical support during feeding time. While I try to remain judgment-free and provide compassionate support as best I can no matter the circumstances, this is a situation where my opinion is so strong, it's hard to contain.

Basically, my opinion is this: if your husband is that hell-bent on the babies being breastfed, he should find a way to grow breasts and lactate. If he can do that and successfully nurse the babies, I give him all the power in the world to scream "I told you so" at the top of his lungs. Until that happens, however, it's fine for him to have an opinion and a desire for things to work a certain way. We all go into parenting with that. But it's imperative that he support you and trust that you know your body and your babies, and that you know what you can handle and what you cannot.

Beyond your husband, any other family members' opinions on whether you breastfeed or not should be left at least three miles from your front door. Okay, I'll climb down off of my soapbox now.

Some moms, and I was one of them, hope to breastfeed their babies, but have to switch gears at some point for one reason or another. Our boys were in the NICU until just over two weeks after their birth. While they were there, I pumped as often as I could so they could get as many of the benefits of breast milk as possible; the hospital supplemented with formula as necessary.

What motivated me to do my best with the antiquated-looking breast pump was knowing I could provide something specifically tailored to Jack's and Henry's physical needs that no other person or formula manufacturer could. I focused on drinking enough each day (beyond what I was sweating out due to the severe hormone drop) to accommodate my determination to give them at least some breast milk at each feeding.

Once our boys came home, I tried hard to breastfeed each baby one or two times per day, and pump just after feedings or in between feedings when possible. After four weeks, I made the decision that, in my case, breastfeeding was no longer doable. I was completely exhausted and could not take another look at that breast pump. Finding time to pump amidst everything else I was trying to do was the straw that broke this very tired camel's back. So, a formula-feeder I became.

Jenna, mom to twin boys Jakob and Noah, intended to breastfeed her babies. Born at thirty-four weeks gestation, they needed her breast milk, or so she believed, more than she needed sleep. However, they arrived so early, their sucking reflex was not yet fully established, so each breastfeeding session took one hour—per baby. "I estimated that I was nursing for seventeen to eighteen hours per day," she remembers. "Amazingly, that lasted for a month, and then they hit a growth spurt. It almost killed me! My mom had the best advice. She reminded me that breast milk or formula was fine—the ultimate goal was happy babies. I listened, and introduced formula. The whole family was better for it."

Some moms choose to feed their babies only formula from day one. Mollie—you remember, the "Ohmigod, how many times a day did you say they were going to eat?" gal— swore up and down before having her boys, Tommy and Kevin, that she'd breastfeed...period...because it was "the healthiest thing for the babies." When the breast pump was wheeled into her room five hours post-delivery, she took one look at it and told the nurse that it was the most unnatural thing she had ever seen. She asked her to please remove it, and requested a few cases of formula be delivered to the room pronto. So, even with the best of intentions, plans change, and that's okay.

Chances are, with more than one baby in the house, some bottle-feeding will be going on—even if it's with breast milk. Chances are also high that, at some point early on, your spouse will be at work or otherwise out of the house, and both babies will need to eat at the same time.

Obviously, a major benefit of bottle-feeding, whether with formula or with pumped breast milk, is that, on occasion (say, at 3:00 a.m.), you get assistance from your husband. I breastfed my daughter, and because I relied on a manual breast pump, I pumped about one quarter of an ounce in fifteen minutes. Therefore, we didn't have much breast milk stored to use in the middle of the night. When she woke up in the middle of the night, I was the only one on-call to actually feed her.

With Jack and Henry, David fed the one who woke first,

allowing me to sleep until the next feeding. Or, he helped with the second baby, which was great. Feeding two babies at the same time when you can't keep your eyes open is an interesting challenge.

There are two schools of thought on whether to bottle-feed babies at the same time or at different times. One professes that it's far easier if your babies eat at different times because you only have to deal with feeding one at a time. Obviously, the downside of this is that you're almost always feeding someone.

The other way of thinking is that it's easiest if they eat simultaneously because that way you only have to do one feeding every few hours, leaving you more time to eat, shower, or—most importantly—sleep (if you're smarter than I was!).

The downside to this approach, if you need to find one, is that feeding two babies at once requires planning. You should certainly decide for yourself which method is easier and abide by it whenever possible. (Sometimes, no matter how hard you try to schedule it, both babies will need to eat at the same time, so it's better to be prepared logistically in advance.)

Strategies for Bottle-Feeding Two Babies at Once

Use Car Seats

Put both babies in their respective car seats next to each other, and hold a bottle in each baby's mouth. (There's no need to buckle them in when they are not mobile unless you're going to pick up the car seat and move it somewhere.) In the beginning, you'll want to burp them halfway through their bottles at a minimum, or you will more than likely be wearing the contents of the entire bottle within fifteen minutes.

When one baby needs to burp, again, there are several methods to choose from. One option is to stop feeding both babies, burp one, burp the other, and start again. Or, if neither baby is patient enough to wait for his sibling's burping marathon to end, another option is to stop feeding both babies momentarily, take one out of his seat, lay him across your thigh, and pat his back while you resume feeding the other one. Then switch and burp the other baby.

Use a Boppy Pillow

While the babies are still under four months of age or so, place them in one Boppy Pillow on the floor and hold bottles in both mouths at the same time. Same strategy on burping applies here as when you feed them in their car seats.

Use Two Couch Pillows

Put a baby's head on each pillow and sit with your legs in a V-shape. Pull the babies in as close to you as possible, and hold a bottle in each baby's mouth.

Use Two Bed Pillows

Put one pillow on your lap with the baby's head on the right side and the body facing left. Then, put the second baby on your right side, with his head next to your right knee and his feet underneath your right arm. Hold a bottle in each baby's mouth. My girlfriend Sonya swore by this approach.

Invest in a Bottle Prop

As mentioned previously, this can be very helpful if you need to feed both babies at once, especially when they get big enough (and wiggly enough) that it's difficult to feed them simultaneously by yourself. The prop isn't meant to substitute for your presence, only to provide you assistance. **Remember never to leave a baby unattended when using a bottle prop in case he chokes.**

I had a horrible time getting my prop to work in the beginning, but when the boys got a bit older, they did much better with it. So, if it doesn't work initially, don't dispose of it. Just keep trying!

Feed Babies from the Same Bottle

This suggestion will probably elicit a big "whammo" from the medical community, but the bottom line is that this book is a guide from moms who've *been* there to moms who are *going* there. Honestly, many moms of twins do this—some in the closet, some publicly—but they're doing it nonetheless.

Barb used to put Olivia and Kambria in their car seats, fill a bottle to six ounces, give one baby an ounce, then the other, and back and forth until they each got enough. This meant fewer bottles to wash and fewer instances where she made a whole bottle, the intended baby ate nothing, and Barb had to pour the contents down the drain.

When Barb admitted to our group that she was doing this, it started the debate over whether to share bottles between babies during the same feeding for fear of spreading germs. Within a week of this discussion, we were all allowing our babies to share bottles—not necessarily by giving one baby an ounce then the other an ounce, and so on, but by feeding one screaming baby who only took an ounce, and then giving the second baby the remainder of the first baby's bottle.

Personally, I decided that Henry's sucking on Jack's cheek while drool ran down it probably spread as many germs as his feeding from the same bottle. If the babies were clearly sick, I did not allow them to share a bottle. It ensured that I could continue to consider myself a responsible parent.

A final benefit of bottle-feeding, and one I didn't figure out until our boys were about four months old, is that you can (and should) make your formula in one big batch—whether the babies are on the same or different formulas. This is more for your mental health than anything else. There will be days when you truly don't think you can mix another bottle, and the ability just to pour it from its container will save your sanity.

Once mixed, the formula is good for forty-eight hours in the refrigerator, so as soon as you know how many ounces you'll need for forty-eight hours, you can mix formula every other *day* as opposed to every other *hour*. In addition, many formulas, when mixed on the spot and shaken vigorously, develop a lot of bubbles that can make a baby's tummy uncomfortable. When you pre-make your formula, those bubbles dissolve while it sits in the refrigerator; once you give your babies their bottles, the formula is bubble-free.

There are many ways to mix the formula. Here are some suggestions.

Strategies for Mixing Formula

Use Tupperware

Get a big Tupperware container, fill it with water to the desired ounce line, add the appropriate amount of powdered formula, and shake vigorously. If your babies are on two different formulas, get two different containers and label them with the "owner's" name.

Use a Formula-Mixing Container

These containers, sold in the baby section of many stores, have a paddle attachment in them that helps dissolve the formula and avoid lumps. Holly is a big fan of this product.

Blend It!

One day, Mollie was sick and tired of shaking and stirring and still seeing lumps in her formula, and she called me. "I've had it. I'm blending!" she said. I had never thought of making formula that way, but I can tell you, I instantly became a proud every-other-day blender of formula.

I also bought this incredible container by SlimLine (I found it at Target, but I've also seen a similar product in the Lillian Vernon catalog). It's about four inches wide but as deep as a standard refrigerator, and it has a spout on it. You fill it with formula (it actually holds about four days' worth, but two days is as long as you can keep pre-made formula before you need to dispose of it) and it takes up the tiniest space in the fridge. When you need to fill a bottle, just put it underneath the spout and pour. It's ingenious. While it's not easy to clean, I managed because I only had to do it every other day.

Some people mix their formula at night or first thing in the morning. (I highly recommend doing it at night. Although you'll be exhausted, if you're lucky, you'll have quiet for a short period of time.) They pour bottles for the next day based on how much their babies are offered at each feeding.

Mollie's babies were always offered between four and eight ounces, depending on their age, so this worked for her. My boys, however, took varying amounts based on when they last ate, what kind of a mood they were in, and possibly, what day of the week it was, so I just poured each bottle as needed. I was still usually still wrong on the amount one way or the other.

One issue that several of us in the "multiples" sorority came up against, and one—even to save our lives—we could not find an answer to, was regarding the digestibility of formula and breast milk given at the same feeding. There was recurring concern that mixing breast milk and formula was causing the babies to have difficulty digesting the concoction. It appeared that, if we did one full feeding of either breast milk or formula and then the next of the other, the babies tolerated it just fine. However, if we combined breast milk and formula into one feeding—either putting both into a bottle or breastfeeding first and supplementing with a bottle of formula (upon discovering a baby didn't get enough, or was screaming so loudly, you knew he still *had* to be hungry)—the baby had difficulty digesting the meal.

In the end, the conclusion of many in the sorority was that you could not combine breast milk and formula into one bottle, and if you breastfed first, you had to will your body to produce enough milk to satisfy the baby for that feeding so that you didn't have to supplement.

I will note that there is no medical reason to not mix formula with breast milk. It is done frequently (and successfully) in the NICU. It was even done for our boys in the NICU; they tolerated it well. Furthermore, many women combine breast milk and formula over the course of the entire first year without it adversely affecting their infants. I just know many of our babies were fussier after a feeding of blended breast milk and formula.

Check with your physician if this issue arises for you, but if you believe the combination of breast milk and formula in one feeding is causing it, know that you are not the first to draw such a conclusion.

According to Dr. Kristine Liberty, a pediatrician in Naperville, Illinois (and my personal hero on many days), some newborns digest breast milk more easily. She notes, "The proteins and/or lactose in some formulas may cause certain infants to experience an increase in gas due to the immaturity of their digestive systems." Often, it might not be the combination of formula and breast milk that is the culprit, but the brand of formula. In this case, a formula change will likely solve the problem.

Dr. Liberty recommends that parents discuss the brand of formula they plan to use with their pediatrician because every infant is different. The discomfort a baby appears to experience after a feeding may not necessarily be a gas-related problem. "A condition known as gastroesophageal reflux affects many infants and may be causing some discomfort," notes Dr. Liberty.

Don't try to self-diagnose your child when it comes to apparent discomfort related to feedings. Let your pediatrician help you work through these issues, which often miraculously fix themselves as the babies grow and their digestive systems mature.

NIGHTTIME FEEDINGS

I'm not asleep, but that doesn't mean I'm awake.
                                    —Author Unknown

One of the challenges that many parents of multiples work hard on (for obvious reasons) is creating a nighttime strategy. David used to get me crazy because, every night at about ten o'clock, he would begin a conversation that went something like this:

David:	Okay, Liz, how should we handle the feedings tonight?
Liz:	What do you mean?
David:	Well, do you want to do the midnight and the four o'clock, and I'll do the two o'clock and the six o'clock?
Liz:	So, you somehow know that not only are they going to wake together for all feedings, but also that they are going to do it at twelve, two, four, and six o'clock?
David:	Well, no, but just to get a general idea of the schedule...
Liz:	David, if I had any general idea of the schedule, don't you think I'd *have* a schedule by now?
David:	Yeah, yeah, so how are we going to do it?

This conversation went around and around (and around) until a baby suddenly started crying, and we began debating who was going to get up. (Of course, David was convinced it should be me since I was apparently penciled in for the midnight feeding. However, I quickly reminded him that we had never successfully *completed* that discussion.) Miraculously, before it got any more heated, the other baby would wake up, the debate was over in a hurry, and we both dragged ourselves to the nursery.

Figuring out your nighttime strategy is critical. It enables you to go into the evening hours with an idea of what to expect and helps you plan your evenings accordingly.

Approaches to Nighttime Feedings

Designate Periods of Time

Designate which of you is responsible for any feeding before 11:00 p.m., and which is responsible from 11:00 p.m. till 4:00 a.m. Whoever was on-call until eleven o'clock goes back on-call at four o'clock. This allows someone to sleep from 8:00 p.m. till 11:00 p.m. (which I could never do, but Mollie did very well), someone to sleep from 11:00 p.m. till 4:00 a.m., and then someone to sleep from 4:00 a.m. till he or she has to get up for work or get up because the *other* is off to work and a baby is crying.

Alternate Feedings

During this phase the babies will usually either wake together to eat or one will wake while the other is eating. Therefore, you can opt to take the first feeding, your husband the second, and on and on. We tried this. The only challenge was that oftentimes a feeding could go on seemingly for hours. One diaper change turned into three, or a baby who had only taken two ounces would suddenly decide he needed more. It is a strategy though, so give it a shot if you think it might work for you.

Play "Baby Roulette"

Also known as "Pick-A-Baby," this option requires you and your husband to each claim a baby. Whenever "your" baby wakes, you're in charge of that feeding and diaper change. Realize, however, that you might have one baby who sleeps better than the other. If you're anything like me, you'll pick the "wrong" baby the first night and switch to the "good" baby the second night, only to discover that they have reversed their roles—and not for the last time! This is definitely the time to have a sense of humor, but I realize it can be tricky at three o'clock in the morning.

Take the Hungry Baby to Another Area of the House

Take the hungry baby downstairs each time he or she needs to eat. Barb and her husband, Tim, did this (which is probably why Barb is in better shape than I am at this point). Tim is a very light sleeper, and to allow him his time in dreamland, Barb fed the girls downstairs in the family room. This worked for her because she could keep the bottles in the refrigerator, heat them in the kitchen, and watch some very interesting infomercials while she fed Olivia and/or Kambria.

Hire a Night Nurse

Admits Charlotte, mom of boy/girl twins, "It would have sounded crazy before having the twins, but if I did it all again, I'd find a way to finance a nighttime nurse for the first three to six months to save my sanity and help with the exhaustion." See the section on The Reality of Sleep Deprivation for more information on this approach.

I truly believe my husband's and my best strategy was the one whereby we designated hours of responsibility. Yes, you will sulk when your shift ends in three minutes and a baby starts to scream. (Do what I did: fake being completely zonked until the clock hits that magic number, and then politely tap your husband on the shoulder and say, "Honey, I'm so sorry, but you're on.") My husband and I got the most consecutive hours of sleep using this strategy. Four hours of sleep a night is not sufficient, true, but four consecutive hours is far better than thirty minutes here and thirty minutes there, totaling four hours. Believe me.

Even with this strategy in place, we tried to be flexible, as best we could. There were nights when one of us was on-call, and the other was painfully aware that our spouse was struggling (in other words, babies screaming so loudly I just knew the police would show up any minute). When this happened, the parent technically off-duty usually marched in and did what he could to assist the other—change a diaper, finish feeding a bottle, whatever—and then marched back to bed.

Another challenge is the preparation of bottles for nighttime feedings. After all, each baby could potentially eat up to four times between 10:00 p.m. and 6:00 a.m. That's a total of eight bottles. There are multiple strategies to choose from.

Nighttime Formula-Feeding Strategies

Organize Your Supplies in One Place

Get a wire basket with handles (the kind you used in college to take to the showers), and stock it with eight bottles filled with water—the number of ounces you calculate each baby will eat per feeding. Take a can of formula or a pre-measured formula container upstairs. This way, when a baby needs to eat, you simply make the formula on the spot. It's at room temperature, so there's no need to warm it.

Put a Refrigerator in Your Room

Not a full-size refrigerator. A dorm-size refrigerator. I sincerely wish we'd done this, and to be honest, if I could go back and do it again, this is one thing I *would* do differently. I'd put the refrigerator in when I was pregnant so that in the middle of the night when I woke up starving, I could grab a pudding, a glass of milk, or a large turkey sub.

You can pre-fill your bottles and store them in the refrigerator, and then use a bottle-warmer to heat them up when a baby is hungry. Sonya's husband, Bob, swears that not only should you have a refrigerator in your room, but a microwave as well, to heat the bottles. Sonya felt this was a bit excessive. The whole topic of warming bottles in the microwave is one we'll get to later, but it's an option if you've got a big bedroom and a crazy husband (no offense, Bob).

Use Ready-to-Feed Formula

Don't forget to take those cute little two-ounce ready-to-feed formula bottles home from the hospital. We left the NICU with a stash of these, and many nights, when my husband or I was so tired we couldn't make out the ounce line on a bottle with our best squinting, they saved us. When the babies are young, they may only take in one or two ounces at a feeding, so these bottles are the perfect size. When they don't finish them—and worse, when they barely take one sip—you want to die as you pour the leftovers down the drain, but...

Several people I know purchased the ready-to-feed formula to use only at night. The problem with this strategy is that the formula—once opened—has to be stored in the refrigerator. So, you're stuck having to get a refrigerator for your room and then heat the bottles, or make trips up and down to the refrigerator several times a night. Also, the ready-to-feed version is quite a bit thicker than the powder. Barb likens the ready-to-feed formula to Slim Fast shakes. Some babies don't tolerate the consistency.

Nighttime Feeding Entertainment

Talk

Regarding the issue I mentioned earlier—not being able to keep your eyes open while doing middle-of-the-night feedings—one solution is to use this time to have a half-coherent conversation with your husband, should he be awake and with you. You could discuss your daily budget, overall long-term financial plan, dream vacation, the fact that you need a bigger home, or the good old days when you slept for twelve hours straight and had so much energy you didn't even get ready to go out until 9:30 p.m.

Sleep

You won't believe how easy it is to nod off during a feeding—and how easy it is to wake up almost instinctively just as your baby finishes his bottle.

Eat

Keep some snacks by the designated feeding area. You will more than likely be feeding a baby only to hear your stomach growling. At that point you will think to yourself, "Gosh, I haven't eaten in a *long* time!" As you continue to focus on this fact in the dark, quiet night, you will get hungrier and hungrier. Again, a psychological thing (as so much of this is). So, keep some snacks nearby.

Whether feeding breast milk or formula, there are several methods for heating bottles. In the beginning, everyone employs the safest method, so start with that (this would be option one or option two listed below). A third (and more controversial) option follows.

Heating Bottles

Use a Large Cup

Fill a big cup with very warm water. Be aware that heating a bottle this way takes several minutes. Mollie used to start heating a bottle when she knew a baby would soon become hungry. She then changed the baby's diaper while the bottle warmed up. By the time his diaper was changed, the bottle was ready. If the bottle gets too warm with this method, dunk it in some cold water for a minute or two.

Use a Commercial Bottle Warmer

Bottle warmers can be purchased at stores like Target or

Babies "R" Us. I used one with my daughter but found that it always over- or under-heated the formula. Barb had great success with the Avent Express Bottle Warmer and never found that it over- or under-heated her bottles.

Use the Microwave

(I want to pull the neck of my shirt up over my head as I suggest this.) Once your babies are a bit older (probably around three months), you'll look for more shortcuts, if for no other reason than for variety.

One option I'm willing to bet you'll wonder about—and hedge on—is using the microwave to warm bottles. By this time, I'm sure you'll make your formula in batches and either pour bottles outright every morning or pour them on demand. Either way, your formula will be cold. Unless your babies couldn't care less (and there are some who couldn't), you'll need to warm the bottles—and fast.

Yes, I know using the microwave to warm formula is a very big no-no according to all the books and healthcare professionals. I understand where they're coming from, but I believe any book written by a mother of twins who advises against it is only doing so out of fear of being criticized by a pediatrician. (And yes, I'm a bit afraid of being criticized by my own at a future appointment.)

Mollie was the last of us to adopt this method of heating bottles. As I've mentioned, she does follow those books to the letter. But when her boys were nearly seven months old, she and her husband took them out of town for the weekend. Out of desperation she warmed their bottles in the microwave, and she never looked back.

A good rule of thumb is five seconds (on high) for every ounce. This depends on your particular microwave, of course. Be sure to invert (not shake) the bottle multiple times once it's been warmed to ensure even distribution of the hot spots. A baby's mouth is much more sensitive to heat and cold than an adult's and burns easily. Also, warm the bottle in the microwave with the nipple off; this allows the heat to escape. If you're nervous about using the microwave for *any* reason, use another method. There's no need for any part of this first year to be any more uncomfortable than it already is!

NOTE: The best way to warm breast milk is by partially submerging the bottle in a large cup of very warm water. ***Do not heat breast milk in the microwave.*** Heating breast milk by microwave has been shown to destroy some of its protective properties.

WORRYING ABOUT A SCHEDULE

Our patience will achieve more than our force.

—Edmund Burke

Undoubtedly, you have been told one too many times that the key to regaining your sanity (and your beauty) is getting the babies on a schedule. This is true, to some degree, but putting too much pressure on yourself too early to accomplish this feat may quickly push your sanity in the wrong direction. Remember, two-week-old babies do not have the ability to go seven hours without eating. They do not have the ability to operate off of a perfectly constructed schedule. And if, by chance, you have miracle babies who have the ability to be on a perfectly reliable schedule from day one, I can almost guarantee that they are not operating on each *other's* perfectly reliable schedule. At least, not yet. They will one day, for sure, and certainly before they are anywhere close to one year old. Be patient. The key here is not to expect too much too soon. Do the best you can and everything will work out just fine.

Start by vowing that you won't allow yourself to feel overwhelmed by the prospect. Start slowly, and by the time your babies are eight or nine months old, they will eat and sleep on the clock. Now, I realize what you are thinking: "Eight or nine months old? I won't *make* it until then!" But you will, and sooner than you think.

Your main goal during this 0- to 3-month period as far as your babies' schedule goes is simply to try to get them on a feeding schedule. Don't worry about nap schedules at this time. Don't worry about nighttimes until the end of this period when you could start introducing a "typical" bedtime depending on your babies' habits and personalities (it might be 8:00 p.m.; it might be 10:00 p.m.). I talk more about napping and nighttime schedules in the 3- to 6-month section, so skip ahead if you like.

Feeding Schedule

Newborn infants do not have an innate feeding schedule. Notes Dr. Liberty, "It is not uncommon for a newborn to feed every one-and-a-half hours. If the mother is breastfeeding, it may seem to her that she is nursing all the time. It is not uncommon for a breastfed infant to nurse for thirty minutes (obviously with twins, that may be a thirty-minute feeding times two if the babies are fed separately), so the interval between feedings may be quite brief. As infants gain weight and mature, they become more efficient with feedings and will be able to tolerate longer stretches between those feedings. I recommend that parents watch for cues from their infants that signal hunger, such as rooting. If the infant nurses or takes the bottle vigorously and seems content afterward, then he was hungry. Many times infants just need a source of non-nutritive sucking, and a pacifier may be a better choice. Eight to twelve feedings in a twenty-four-hour period is recommended for the newborn."

Honestly, if you can get your babies onto a reliable feeding schedule before they hit three months of age, you should write your own book on how to do that alone. So often, twins are born prematurely and simply take longer to reach a point where they can reliably take a consistent amount at consistent intervals. During these early months, it will also be difficult for you to feel comfortable proclaiming with confidence that the baby who has been screaming for two hours and seemingly eating for three is *definitely* not hungry.

The best approach is to try to establish set feeding times for your babies. Try to get them to eat every three hours or every four hours, whichever seems to work best in your situation. Realize that the babies will go through several growth spurts during these three months. (Fair warning: you will question whether they are going through a growth spurt during this time as frequently as you will question whether they are teething in later months.) Those spurts will require that they feed more frequently for a few days. By the time you have nearly given up on establishing a feeding schedule, and are sure you have tried everything, the babies will hit that three-month mark. It truly becomes easier (the feeding part, at least) once this occurs.

According to Dr. Liberty, infants develop better sleeping habits when their hunger cycles are regulated. "Parents can encourage a routine by offering feedings at regular intervals. They may also encourage more predictable sleeping habits by putting their infants down to sleep at regular times. Newborns may initially sleep for only twenty to sixty minutes at a time, however the length of their 'naps' will increase by the time they are four to six months old, as their sleep cycles mature."

THE DOORBELL THAT KEEPS RINGING

My evening visitors, if they cannot see the clock, should find the time in my face.

—Ralph Waldo Emerson

About as certain as it is that you'll feel like your babies eat more frequently than the second hand on the clock ticks is the fact that your doorbell will ring almost as frequently (and hopefully not *more* frequently). During this time, everyone wants to help. The problem is, not everyone's definition of help matches your own.

Lots of times people think they're helping by popping in to take care of the babies while you cook or clean. The reality is that you really need someone to do the unpleasant (and hard-on-the-body) tasks of cooking, cleaning, laundry, or grocery shopping while *you* feed the babies, change them, feed them again, change them again, and with any luck, sneak in a fifteen-minute nap for yourself.

Traffic Control

Ask Visitors to Knock

Place a PLEASE KNOCK sign on your front door. Place it on top of or directly above or below the doorbell so there's little chance of any literate person missing it. Inevitably, you will have just gotten a baby to sleep after hours and hours of rocking, singing, and/or bouncing only to have someone ring the doorbell. Also inevitable is that this same person who is oblivious enough to ring the bell will also be oblivious enough to ring it two or three times in a row—just in case you didn't hear it the first time (or to signal their extreme excitement).

Request Provisions

If the visitors are people who will be coming over frequently—grandparents, aunts, uncles—ask them if they wouldn't mind bringing a package of diapers or a dinner with them when they come. At this stage, it's a trade—if you bring sustenance or other necessities, you're welcome to visit with our babies.

Be Honest

Be sure to let visitors know what *you* need. Don't feel

obligated to give in to *their* needs. Let them know if you really need someone to come and do laundry or the dishes or prepare a meal since you haven't eaten in two days. Try to make it clear up-front that these visits early on aren't so much to take care of the babies as they are to take care of you, which enables you to care for the babies.

Keep Germs at Bay

Make sure everyone washes their hands before handling the babies.

Stick to Your Routine

If you've managed to create even the smallest semblance of a schedule—or even if you just want to *think* you have for your mental health—do *not* feel you should deviate from it to accommodate visitors. If the babies are napping when visitors arrive and don't wake up until after they leave, apologize and mention that you hope they'll come back when the babies are awake.

If visitors call ahead of time, let them know when you think the babies *might* be awake, but remember that in the early weeks, although visitors will undoubtedly want to see the babies, what you really need is help.

Take Care of Yourself

At any point, if your idea of help is just to turn your babies over to a trusted friend or family member, by all means do so. Even someone sitting with them while you take a nap might feel like the greatest vacation you've had in years.

BATHING

Creativity can solve almost any problem. The creative act, the defeat of habit by originality, overcomes everything.

—George Lois

This activity has never been one of my favorites. I know a lot of parents love their children's bath time and find it an incredible opportunity for bonding while the babies play in the water. I have personally never felt that way. It's always been an in-wash-out activity. Even when my daughter was an infant, bathing her was not one of my favorite activities, and I only had *one* baby to contend with. But, because I had only one child to bathe, it was something I did regularly and quickly. With the boys, that wasn't the case.

First, there were two of them (obviously). Second, I had a toddler running around, and I couldn't leave her alone while I bathed the boys. Third, making two trips up and down the stairs to get the boys to the bathroom left me with little energy to do the actual bathing. And last, bending over the bathtub—not once, but twice—left me in need of a chiropractor (but, of course, with no time to see one).

Here are some easy ways to make bath time pleasant. First and foremost, always wait until your babies' umbilical cords have fallen off, and if applicable, your sons' circumcisions have healed before you submerge them in water. Until those two things have occurred, give sponge baths as needed, especially around their bottoms and necks (where formula has undoubtedly found a home and turned into cottage cheese).

My strongest advice for bathing two babies, especially if you have other children—but even if you don't—is to use the downstairs bathroom or kitchen sink. Until the boys were at least three months old, I bathed them one at a time in the powder room sink because it was smaller, and I felt I had more control over their slippery little bodies. Once they got too big for the bathroom sink, I moved to the kitchen sink.

Using the sinks as bathtubs proved indispensable for several reasons. First, the height was perfect. No more bending over and bothering an already sore lower back. Second, everything I needed was right at arm's length. And finally, the space was compact so the boys felt secure, and my toddler was always within earshot if not eyesight.

One thing to take note of is whether you have a draft coming through your kitchen or bathroom. If you do, turn off all ceiling fans and close all windows while giving baths. My boys were literally in, washed, and out in about ninety seconds, so the opportunity for getting chilled was extremely low.

Additional Strategies for Bathing Young Babies

Be Organized

For starters, always make sure your supplies are at arm's length and ready for use before you begin bathing. Have your baby shampoo (I highly recommend a body wash that cleans both their hair and their body), towel, washcloth, cotton balls, and so forth, out and ready. It's been said a million times, but just so I know I've put it out there, ***never leave your baby unattended in the tub or sink for even a second.*** Babies have drowned in as little as an inch of water.

Use the Tub-in-a-Tub Approach

If you're not as vertically challenged as I am, try putting a baby bathtub inside your own bathtub and bathe them one at a time. Find a baby bathtub with a little drain in it because you can drain the soapy water out and then refill with clean water without having to lift and dump a heavy, water-filled baby tub.

You can put a baby bath sponge inside the baby bathtub. These inexpensive sponges fit the length of the tub and keep babies from slipping around. They are also wonderful to use when you're doing those initial sponge baths. Put them on your floor or counter (never leave the baby unattended while doing this), and they have a soft cushion to lie on as they get their sponge bath.

Bathe with Your Baby

Depending on the baby's size, it may work (especially

toward the end of the first three-month period) to bring one baby into the bathtub with you, clean him, and then hand him to your husband who will dry him, clothe him, and hand you the next baby. This is a more time-consuming way to do baths, but it can be a fun, bonding experience if you are in a bonding mood or looking for something fun to do on a Friday night. (I know, every night is Friday night, or Monday night, or Wednesday night...)

Utilize Hospital Supplies

Mollie put a small pink basin she "borrowed" from the hospital on her kitchen table. This gave her a small tub at waist level. Her husband held one of the babies in the water and she did the washing. Then they bathed the second baby. When the bath was finished, she used cotton balls to apply baby oil to make the babies' skin soft. That is, until she discovered the miracle of baby oil gel, a product that provides the same benefit with less sliminess than baby oil.

UNSOLICITED ADVICE:
STORIES FROM THE TRENCHES

It's so simple to be wise. Just think of something stupid to say, and then don't say it.

—Sam Levenson

I have great passion for this topic. I could write an entire book on the comments you are likely to entertain, the questions you are likely to be asked, and ways—polite or otherwise—you are likely to respond (depending on your hormone level, how tired you are of that question, and your niceness quotient). People can comment until the cows come home about how you should be doing this or should not be doing that, but when the day is done, they will go home (hopefully), and you will do things the way you see fit.

Some of the most problematic people from whom to receive unsolicited advice is family, yours or your husband's. In most cases, these folks are merely trying to help, but the reality is that their comments frequently leave you feeling inadequate, unprepared, and possibly angry. The best way to deal with this is to stay as calm as possible. The last thing you need at this time is a big hoopla over something that, in the end, no one has control over but you.

Many people's families are nothing but helpful after the babies are born. They cook, clean, wash clothes, shop, and do whatever else is needed. Some are even available in the middle of the night! Unfortunately, not everyone is lucky enough to have this experience. If you are one of those people, don't worry, we're going to get you through it.

When her mother-in-law suggested for the umpteenth time that she hold the babies while the new mom made lunch for everyone, one of my friends handled the situation brilliantly. She enthusiastically said, "Thanks, I've got it covered" (as she reached for the babies, biting her bottom lip and silently reminding herself, "I passed the test on whether I could handle twins when I proved I could handle *you*").

If the offenders won't back off, curtail visits (have your husband answer the phone) until they get it (not likely); until Dr. Phil is available for a house call to help them "get real" about what they are doing (again, not likely); or until you are better rested, more confident in your parenting, and otherwise better able to deal with them.

Questions and comments from perfect strangers are a different ballgame. You won't believe how interested they can be, both in the babies' conception and your parenting. I couldn't believe how many people asked if our twins were conceived using fertility drugs. No one ever asked if my daughter was conceived using fertility drugs. Now, if I had been pregnant with nine babies, chances are high that I used infertility treatments (though I believe a woman in China recently gave birth to spontaneous sextuplets).

Twins are more and more common nowadays—not only because of the increased use and availability of infertility treatments, but because women are waiting until later in life to conceive, which increases the potential for them to drop more than one egg per cycle. It shocks me that so many people still believe you have to be on fertility drugs to conceive two babies at once.

Here are some of the more common questions you are sure to be asked, or comments you are sure to receive, along with my humble opinions on the reasons for these questions and comments. So you are not left completely hanging, I've provided a variety of responses to have at-the-ready. One issue that's interesting to work through is when to bite your tongue and when to just let it rip. This also applies, of course, to meddling by family members.

Handling the Curiosity

Are They Twins?

Barb and her husband, Tim, were asked on numerous occasions if their newborn girls were twins. Tim was dying to say, "No, this one is two weeks older."

Jack and Henry look so different from one another that I am constantly asked if they are both mine. When I answer "Yes," the inquirer inevitably asks how many months apart they are. I want to say, "You realize that there would have to be at least a nine month age difference between them for that question to get a genuine answer. Do they look like they were born nine months apart?" Different? Yes. Nine months different? No. I even had a woman inquire as to whether my boys were "those kinds of twins you hear about who have two different fathers." Lovely.

One day, Jenna's husband had had enough of strangers asking if his sons, identically dressed and clearly the same age, were twins. He responded to the next inquirer with, "No, Jakob is my son and Noah is my wife's. We met online."

Mollie was in the mall one day when a woman came up to her and asked if her boys were twins (although fraternal twins, they are each other's clone, so this question was semi-ridiculous to begin with). Mollie said "Yes," and the woman said she assumed that Tommy was the older one because he was bigger. Mollie commented that actually Kevin was older. The woman said, "Oh—by how many weeks?" Again, where do you even go with that?

What Kind of Fertility Drugs Did You Take?

Never, *never*, will I understand how people feel comfortable asking others—especially perfect strangers—this question. I've decided that it's all in the name of insane curiosity about how others live their lives. Perhaps they are really bored, are unnaturally curious other people's personal lives, or are poorly affected by the way the stars and moon aligned the previous night. Never have I had someone actually going through infertility treatment ask me about my experiences with the challenge. Most people going through these personal and private procedures are just as reserved as I am on the topic, if not more so.

All that being analyzed and pointed out, the time comes to move on and attempt to find a comfortable response. Some moms are open and honest about the way they got pregnant, and want to share it with the world. (I don't know any of these moms, but they probably exist.) If you are such a person and some stranger on the street seems oh-so-interested in the "how" of your pregnancy, then by all means open up and give them every gory detail.

But one of my favorite responses is to say, "Oh, are you having trouble getting pregnant?" People are usually not nearly as comfortable answering this question as they were in asking their initial one, so this often ends the whole discussion in a hurry.

Another option is to respond, while wearing the biggest smile you can muster, "Why do you want to know?" You would be positively amazed by how many questioners have no *clue* why they want to know and simply move on.

A final favorite response of mine is to smile and say "Wow, that's a really personal question!" (then just keep walking). It's like saying, "None of your bleeping business!" with the nice tone that a mother of twins should use.

If your hormones are in overdrive, respond the way one hilarious friend of mine did. When asked by a cashier whether she had taken fertility drugs to conceive her twins, she responded, "No, we just had a lot of sex." That was the end of that!

Did You Know You Were Having Twins?

Nowadays, many parents of twins can't believe a woman can find out she is expecting twins at the time of delivery. Many women who've undergone infertility treatments learn of their double blessing early in their pregnancies. In other cases, the doctor may suspect a multiple pregnancy if a woman suffers from excessive morning sickness or has abnormally high hormone levels in her blood. Many parents receive the news of their multiple gestation at their twenty-week ultrasound when two babies are detected.

Tony and Rochelle, who live in Ohio, had quite a different experience. Rochelle had an internal ultrasound at the beginning of her pregnancy as well as a more thorough ultrasound at twenty weeks gestation. The only surprise news Tony and Rochelle received at the twenty-week ultrasound was the sex of one baby. They hadn't wanted to know, and the doctor inadvertently blurted it out. Somehow, in the midst of feeling flustered that he'd accidentally ruined the surprise, he "missed" the other baby.

When Rochelle inquired why she was getting so big, the doctor commented that she was simply carrying a big baby. Toward the end of her pregnancy, Rochelle often wondered how big her baby could be—it was simultaneously kicking her in the ribs and pelvic floor!

They were in for quite a shock. "At 37.5 weeks, my wife woke me up at 4:00 a.m. because she was experiencing severe back pain. She took a shower, and we waited until 5:00 to call our doctor. We were told to go to the hospital and be checked. As the nurse was hooking up the fetal heart monitor, she asked if we were expecting twins. We informed her that we were not. She told us that she thought she heard an echo of the baby's heartbeat. She left the room and returned with another monitor and told us that they should beat at about the same rate. They were a few beats off.

"To make a long story short, after a quick ultrasound and physical, we were informed that my wife was dilated to ten centimeters, having twins, scheduled for a C-section, and that things would move quickly. Within a half hour of being informed that Rochelle was pregnant with twins, our sons were born."

Which Side of Your Family Do Twins Run On?

This is usually a harmless question, and while you will become royally irritated by it, I find that most people who ask it are genuinely trying to make polite conversation. They are typically not the same people who ask what fertility drugs you took, or what fancy position you and your husband "did it" in to conceive multiples.

When people ask about twins running on one side or the other of our family, I usually comment that they run on neither side. Few people understand that twins only "run" on the mother's side, since only the mother passes the tendency to naturally release more than one egg to her daughter. Though I'm sure they'd love to claim otherwise, a man's sperm is not strong or appealing enough to force a woman's ovary to release another egg. Identical twins have nothing to do with genetics. An egg splitting is still considered a purely random act.

Another popular question along these same lines is, "Do twins run in your family?" In this day and age, the answer to this, even if you're willing, often requires more time than you'll have. Plus, if they "run in your family" because the person who had them did not have spontaneous twins, but instead relied upon infertility treatments, you may need diagrams for those who require visual explanations. The bottom line is that "Yes" or "No" is usually the best answer. Pick one. Pick a different one each day if you want. Or be creatively smart like Carole, a mom of triplets, and reply "They do now!"

Wow, I'm Sure Glad It's You and Not Me!

Hate this one! It's just so unnecessary, and as my mother always says, "If you have nothing nice to say, don't say anything at all." Some people just feel they *have* to say something—I have no idea why—so they say something relatively stupid. Do not waste a moment on these folks. Here are two options: put on your best half-smile and keep walking, or comment as nicely (or as cynically) as you would like, "Me, too!"

How Do You Do It?

Okay—another one of my not-so-favorites. But here's what I've come to dissect from this comment. When people ask, "How do you do it?" they don't really want an answer; this is their translation for "*I* couldn't do it." And clearly they could not, or they'd have twins with them as well. Nevertheless, I'm willing to acknowledge that in all likelihood—albeit subconsciously—they are paying me a compliment. They are saying, "I could not do it. You *are* doing it. You are an amazing human being who I wish I had the fortitude to call my friend." Therefore, I've taken to accepting this statement simply as a poorly worded compliment. I usually respond (so I'm not totally rude to these kind, complimentary folks) with, "Oh, they make it easy."

If, however, you are having a particularly bad day, answer

his or her question by going on and on, beginning with, "Well, I get up around 6:30 a.m., go downstairs and get breakfast ready for the troops, then fly like Mary Poppins back up the steps, and sneak silently into their room to pick out their coordinating outfits for the day. I subsequently slide down the banister and skip into the family room to ensure that all the videos, books, and other learning toys are lined up and ready to go…" By this point, the questioner is trying to get away from *you*.

But there was the day when nothing had gone right, and I was sure bedtime would never arrive. A woman with whom I was sharing an elevator sighed and said, as though just thinking about my day made her as tired as I already felt, "How on *earth* do you do it?" I looked at the woman, at the boys, and back at the woman to say, "You know what? I don't have any idea!"

You Aren't Going to Have Any More…Are You?

Jenna, mother of twin boys, could not believe it when people asked her if she and her husband planned to have more children—when the boys were only four and a half months old. She commented, "We usually shut them up with, 'Yeah, this time we're going to try for twin girls.' Sometimes we tell them that we'd like another set of twin boys so that we can field half a baseball team!"

You Sure Do Have Your Hands Full.

Again, a real original comment and one you're likely to receive at least seven times a week, depending on how frequently you get out. It's really just a not-so-clever combination of "How do you do it?" and "I'm glad it's you and not me." Folks who utter this are simply not comfortable with awkward silences. Just smile, and let your mood on a particular day determine how broadly or faintly you deliver that smile.

Which One is Smarter?

I'm still speechless over that one, though I've only been asked it once!

The braver women of the world (or perhaps those in a really sour state) conjure up brazen responses to some of these comments and questions. One example, uttered by a woman in our Marvelous Multiples class with whom we unfortunately lost contact, still makes me chuckle.

She was grocery shopping with her husband one afternoon when she was about six months pregnant with her twins. The woman behind her in line overheard her talking with her husband about the babies. This woman actually followed her out of the store, hailed her down, and asked if she had been on fertility drugs. To this, the pregnant woman responded, "Excuse me. Did I ask you if you douche?" I about fell out of my chair when I heard this. It's definitely the extreme way of saying, "That's a really personal question and none of your business," but after all the inappropriate questions we've each been asked, my girlfriends and I have gained more and more respect for that woman's guts.

A woman approached me and my sons as we walked to their physical therapy appointment at the hospital one morning. She commented on how cute they were, and how *big* they were (my husband is 6' 6"). She asked how early they'd been born, how much they weighed at birth, you know, all the stuff people are fascinated with for reasons unbeknownst to mothers of multiples. She asked if they were breastfed and I said, "No." She looked at me and said, rather condescendingly, "They're *not?*" I said, "No, they're not." Nose up, eyes down, as if she were providing me with valuable information that would change the course of history, she said, "Well, you *can* breastfeed two, you know." I should have said, "Oh, how old are your twins?" but I'm simply never ready for these people at the moment they strike, so I just said, "Well, *technically*, you can, yes," and made a beeline for the therapy room.

Holly, you'll remember, has triplet girls, and, of course, has gotten numerous comments about funding three college educations *and* three weddings. But the strangest comment she ever got was from a woman who actually said, to Holly's husband, Paul, "Wow. Imagine how much you guys are going to be spending on tampons in twelve years!" That one left them both with their jaws on the floor.

The strangest question I ever got was from a man who didn't ask if my boys were identical (which they clearly are not), what their names were, or whether I had used infertility drugs, but, instead, inquired as to how many minutes apart they were at birth. I was struck by his question because no one had ever asked me anything quite like this. I actually had to say, "Excuse me?" I then told him they were twenty-eight minutes apart, and he wanted to know who was born first. I told him, and that was the end of that. Still intrigues me to this day.

Finally, there's Terri. Twenty-two weeks along with her twins, she was approached by a woman who thought she might like to know she was now a member of the group with the highest divorce rate. Really, people, what is the world coming to?

Clearly you need to be prepared for unsolicited questions and advice left and right until, certainly, your kids reach eighteen. I'm already prepared for, "Are they in the same class?" along with the questioner's unsolicited opinion on the pros and cons. Or, "Do they have different friends?" and on and on. I'll probably always be unprepared in the moment, but at least in hindsight, I hope to have some good responses to share with my friends.

THE EFFECT OF YOUR LIFE AT THE SINK

In this business, you can never wash the dinner dishes and say they are done. You have to keep doing them constantly.

         —Mary Wells Lawrence

You probably can't believe you'll create more dirty dishes than when your babies are drinking formula every three to four hours. But just wait until they start eating solid food! Don't worry; we have a couple of chapters left to go before we get there. Doing all those dishes, however, made my hands, and most of my girlfriends' hands, look and feel like fish scales before we had our "aha" moments and did the following. Start these practices from the beginning and your hands will only age a year in the next twelve months as opposed to ten years in two weeks.

Maintaining Age-Appropriate Hands

Do as Little Hand-Washing as Possible

Ensure that you have enough bottles and nipples to last you twenty-four hours without washing. This is worth the extra money (though it's not really that much extra). Wash all bottles/nipples in the dishwasher nightly, even if there are only three nipples and two bottles. You will feel so much better not having to unload a stuffed dishwasher each morning, yet still starting each day with a clean supply.

Use Rubber Gloves

Be sure to invest in a pair of rubber gloves for washing dishes that cannot wait until that nightly dishwasher run. Otherwise, within about three weeks, your hands will be so chapped you'll want to die. For our first holiday gift-exchange after our babies were born, the sorority all exchanged bottles of lotion!

Use Lotion—Often

Have a bottle of lotion by your kitchen sink and apply it after each handwashing. Some of the thicker lotions— Eucerin, Cook's Lotion by Crabtree & Evelyn, or No-Crack® Day-Use Super Hand Crème (I get mine at Restoration Hardware)—have been my favorites.

LAUNDRY, LAUNDRY, AND MORE LAUNDRY

I believe you should live each day as if it is your last, which is why I don't have any clean laundry, because, come on, who wants to wash clothes on the last day of their life?

—Unknown

Here's my most important piece of advice for this challenge: beyond what's necessary to get something to stay on the hanger, don't button anything before putting it away. Unless your name is Holly.

One night, a few of us went over to Holly's house to watch her triplets so she and her husband could get out for a few hours. She brought down their "nighttime onesies" (these were exactly the same as the daytime onesies, only "clean"). The girls' pajamas were completely buttoned and even, I believe, ironed. (By the way, we also learned then that Holly had created bar graphs to depict the girls' eating patterns over the first couple of months. Each girl had a different-colored line on the graph. Holly was using this graph to ensure none of them developed eating habits severely opposed to the others. That about says it.)

She's a personality type I don't believe has been officially identified yet—like A+ or something—but that's the kind of person God gives triplets to. Otherwise, I truly believe at least one of them would disappear under the sofa for a month or two.

One day, I asked Barb when on earth she had time to

wash the sheets on her bed (for some strange reason, we only had one set of sheets at the time). "Well, I haven't had time to change them for two weeks," she responded. "So today at Target, I just threw a new set into the cart."

"But don't you need to wash *those* before you put them on the bed?" I asked.

"I don't," she declared.

If worse comes to worst, use the motto I frequently use when heading for the airport: "Always take your driver's license and credit card so you can get through security, but buy whatever you've forgotten on the other end" (or in this case, don't have time to wash).

Additional Laundry Solutions

Storing of Dirty Clothes

Put dirty clothes in the laundry room so you don't have to stare at them spilling over the laundry basket in the babies' room, and run laundry when you have a free minute. If it doesn't make you nervous, designate the laundry to your husband. (I've also found that God doesn't give twins to mothers with incapable husbands, so I feel confident your husband will be able to take care of some daily tasks. In fact, a recent Babycenter.com poll revealed that 97 percent of moms surveyed believe their partners are parenting as well as they are, so there you go.)

Stain Removal

For stain removal, try Mother's Miracle, Clorox 2, and/or Biz. We've each had great success with all these products.

Sheet Protectors

Save frequent sheet changes by putting sheet protectors in the cribs (the kind that go over the sheet). There are narrow ones that became ineffective once the babies start moving around (I always worried that Jack would get his head wedged between the sheet protector and the sheet), and larger ones that cover the whole crib sheet.

Also, as mentioned in the Gear section, get a mattress protector that fits like a pillowcase over the mattress. This way, when you change the sheet, you don't pull off the mattress protector every time you pull off the sheet.

ENDLESS DIAPERS

If we couldn't laugh, we would all go insane.

—Jimmy Buffett

The only thing more voluminous than the baby clothes you accumulate the first year is the number of diapers you dispose of each day. You'll need a receptacle at-the-ready for the all-important job of containing them until the trashman comes.

We recommend using the Playtex Diaper Genie, Baby Trend Diaper Champ, or some such product initially. Many people keep one upstairs and one downstairs. However, with more than one baby, it's going to fill up *fast!* Many people I know (except Mollie, but again, she's often the exception) quickly established an alternative (and larger) disposal unit, such as a large, lidded trash can designated the "diaper can" in the garage.

While you're still changing diapers during the night, keep a Diaper Genie upstairs and a trash can inside your garage for your daytime changes. (When the diapers get bigger and you're changing less during the night, you'll probably get rid of the Genie and simply put them all outside.)

COMMON EVERYDAY PROBLEMS

Everybody gets so much information all day long that they lose their common sense.

—Gertrude Stein

With the availability of the Internet, so much information is available to each of us on any given subject that we could, if we chose, spend eons researching, and finding possible reasons for, the pimples that have developed on our newborn's face, remedies for gas pains, and myriad solutions for diaper rash. New moms of twins simply don't have the time to do this level of research! Therefore, I asked Dr. Liberty to help with questions related to common, more medically-based, newborn challenges that all the sorority sisters had day-in and day-out. Here are some of her insights.

Gas

"Gas pain is a common problem in newborns. Many times, an infant will draw his or her legs up to the abdomen when gas pain is present. Parents may want to try gentle rocking or use an infant swing or vibrating chair to alleviate gas. Infant massage or laying the baby across your lap on his or her belly may also help.

Over-the-counter infant gas relief drops may be helpful; however, a phone call to your pediatrician first is advisable. It is possible that a formula change may be helpful as well, but parents should discuss this approach with their pediatrician before making the decision themselves. If gas is a frequent problem, I would encourage parents to discuss it with their doctor. Prolonged crying during which an infant appears inconsolable may be a sign of something more worrisome, and parents should consult their physician."

Diaper Rash

"Many pediatricians recommend against the use of diaper creams in the newborn period. Frequently a diaper rash during the first four to six weeks of life will improve by using a gentle cleanser or plain water to clean the diaper area.

Leaving the diaper area open to air for periods of time is often helpful as well.

A yeast rash is common when infants/toddlers are in diapers. Usually the irritation/redness appears in the folds of skin in the diaper area and often around the scrotum on little boys. This type of rash does not always resolve with traditional over-the-counter diaper creams. Parents should talk to their physicians about an anti-yeast cream. Any blistering, bleeding, or persistent rash in the diaper area usually requires additional therapies. In this case, the infant's doctor may have the family use two or more creams simultaneously."

Constipation

"Intermittent constipation can occur in newborn infants. Breastfed infants may only have bowel movements every few days. Sometimes parents perceive this as constipation. If the stools are soft and passed easily, it is not constipation. Difficulty passing stools from birth may signal a more significant problem and an evaluation by a physician is recommended."

Spitting Up

"Newborns may spit up frequently due to gastroesophageal reflux. This condition results from a weakness in the muscle that separates the stomach from the esophagus. As a result, stomach contents pass more easily into the esophagus, often resulting in spitting up. Most infants outgrow this condition without any intervention (approximately 50 percent by six months and 90 percent by nine months).

Frequent spitting up is of concern when the infant is not gaining weight or seems to be fussy/irritable between feedings. Projectile vomiting is also of concern and warrants an evaluation by the baby's physician."

Baby Acne

"Neonatal acne is a response to maternal androgens. It usually occurs between two and four weeks of age and may persist for the first four to six months. It consists of inflammatory (red) pinpoint marks on the skin, mixed with tiny pustules (pimples). Neonatal acne occurs mainly on the face and scalp. Treatment varies depending on the severity. Gentle cleansing of the skin is recommended, as abrasive cloths or harsh detergents will make the condition worse. Acne can be treated with mild anti-inflammatory creams."

Cradle Cap

"Cradle Cap (Seborrheic Dermatitis) occurs commonly in infants. It is due to an overproduction of sebum and results in a shiny appearance on the scalp with a collection of scales adherent to the scalp. The scales may appear white to yellow in color.

Cradle cap improves with frequent hair washing and gentle exfoliation using an infant hairbrush, soft toothbrush, and/or the pad of your finger. (It's okay to exfoliate over the soft spot.) For more severe cases, you can use a dandruff shampoo, but be careful to avoid the eye area. Baby oil may be rubbed into the scalp to help loosen the scale."

Dry Skin

"At birth, a full-term newborn's skin is usually soft and smooth. Within a few days the skin will start to appear dry and cracked, especially around the ankles and wrists, due to the shedding of the stratum corneum, which accumulates before the infant is born. During this process, topical lotions can be used to hydrate the skin."

One of the benefits of having a friend or two with multiples is that you can use each other's pediatricians (not literally, of course, unless you've got unbelievable health insurance and a lot of free time on your hands, but you can use these resources without actually visiting their offices).

Within our "multiples" sorority, we see between three and four pediatric groups, with one to three of us using the same group. When one or both of our babies has gotten sick or had another issue such as gas or cradle cap, it's been interesting to call each other and find out what advice the others' pediatricians have given for the same ailment.

The pediatric group I use is what I consider medically-focused. More often than not, they have a medicinal solution rather than a holistic or natural one. Barb's pediatrician, on the other hand, is more holistically focused; she does use medicine, especially in the case of a raging infection that requires antibiotics, but for the less-problematic stuff, she likes to try something natural first.

When Jack had a horrible case of baby acne, our pediatrician recommended a 1 percent hydrocortisone cream, while Barb's pediatrician recommended using a washcloth to gently dab her daughter Olivia's face with diluted chamomile tea. The approach of Barb's pediatrician became a running joke because, before long, it seemed she was prescribing diluted chamomile tea for everything from baby acne to constipation. Often, however, it did just as good a job as the medicinal solution I received (though not in the case of baby acne).

The bottom line is, if you have a pediatrician you trust and you trust your girlfriends as well, none of the solutions is likely to be harmful (provided the pediatrician actually attended medical school!). Having different solutions and different perspectives only makes you feel more in control. Run alternative solutions by your own doctor if it makes you feel better.

Barb's pediatrician has a carrot soup recipe she swears by as a cold remedy. Barb does now as well, because her girls were better within two days of ingesting it (at eight weeks of age). My boys still had their colds a week later, taking four to six doses of PediaCare a day.

NURTURING SIBLINGS

A human being should be able to change a diaper, plan an invasion, butcher a hog, conn a ship, design a building, write a sonnet, balance accounts, build a wall, set a bone, comfort the dying, take orders, give orders, cooperate, act alone, solve equations, analyze a new problem, pitch manure, program a computer, cook a tasty meal, fight efficiently...
—Excerpt from the notebooks of Lazarus Long
from Robert Heinlein's *Time Enough for Love*

I love this quote because if you substitute "a mom" for "a human being," it creates an accurate representation of the myriad roles moms play on a minute-by-minute basis (though I've yet to conn a ship, whatever that means, or butcher a hog).

Many twins are born to parents who have no other children. Yet just as often, it seems, twins are born to parents with at least one other child. One of the most common concerns I hear from expectant or new moms of twins is, "How will I ensure that my older child doesn't feel left out?" Parents often harbor strong concern over how to adjust to meet the needs of all their children, and to ensure that their older children don't feel displaced by the simultaneous arrival of two siblings.

When Jack and Henry were born, Grace had just turned two. This was both a good age and a bad age to introduce siblings to her. Good because she was really too young to understand what was happening to her life or to feel displaced by the boys (though I hear with frequency that this has more to do with the fact that she's a girl). Bad because she was two!

She was still in diapers, still learning to define herself and assert her independence, and still dependent on David and me for everything from playing with her and showing her how much we loved her to getting her dressed and cleaning up after her (though, amazingly, she did learn how to work the TV, the remote, and the VCR by herself almost immediately after the boys came home).

I cannot tell you how many people asked me, "How much harder is it to parent newborn twins with a two-year-old?" At the time, I was as amazed to report as they were to hear, "It isn't bad at all."

She ignored the boys for the first six months. Then they turned six months old, she turned two-and-a-half, and I no longer said how easy it was to have a toddler as well as twins. She wanted to interact with the boys, but she didn't understand why she couldn't tackle a six month old. She wanted to feed them, but didn't understand why they couldn't eat her pretzels. At this point, I think she started to feel the blow of their presence in terms of the attention and time they took away from her.

The situation became difficult in a hurry. As much as I wanted to spend time with each child, reality had to be addressed: I had three children under the age of three and only twenty-four hours in a day. I did my best to spend quality time with Grace in the evenings—often taking her with me on shopping trips to the grocery or Target—or scheduled time with her during the boys' rest time, or put a puzzle together or played "Hide and Go Peek" with her before bedtime. But, sometimes during the boys' rest time, I needed her to rest because *I* needed to rest.

Things were the most difficult when Grace turned three. Happily, my husband showed up one evening with a new book for me entitled *Parenting Your Strong-Willed Child*, by Rex Forehand, Ph.D. and Nicholas Long, Ph.D. This gift beat any large-carat-weight diamond at that point. I read that book and did exactly as it recommended. I remained calm as I informed Grace for the forty-third time that it was naptime, even if she didn't want to nap. I remained consistent; I didn't allow myself to give in when she begged for M&Ms in the checkout aisle—even though I knew I could stop her shrieking by simply handing her that magic little brown bag. I identified as many daily opportunities as I could for Grace and me to spend time together, just the two of us. I encouraged her in the moments when she chose a positive approach to getting what she wanted, and helped her identify alternate solutions during the times when her approach wasn't appropriate and, therefore, unsuccessful. I reminded myself over and over again that she was simply at an age when she was testing her boundaries. It was my job to show her what the boundaries were, and stick to them so that she knew what to expect (even if she didn't like it). I did the best I could. And that's all any of us can do. We acknowledge the situation for what it is, and then we do what we can to fix it.

If you find yourself in a similar situation, use the resources available to you. If you find time, read (or skim) books on dealing with the dilemma. Invite one of your child's friends over for an hour or so to play every once in a while. If you have relatives nearby, ask them to come over and play, or see if you can take your older child there to play for a few hours.

The most important thing to do for your older children during your pregnancy, and especially after the babies' birth, is to continue making them feel important and loved. I know what you're thinking—Duh! The most successful thing I did ahead of time was stock up on some coloring books, puzzles, and other small, inexpensive items I could pull out in a hurry. If Grace was feeling left out, and I had to feed a baby (again), I could pull out a new little "gift," which got her so excited that she forgot how left out she felt. These "gifts" weren't bribes. They were merely temporary distractions.

It's also important to nurture the relationships between your older child and the babies, though this may be a slow-going process. How well and how quickly the relationship begins to cement itself depends on many factors—how old your older child is, how secure he or she feels, etc. Don't expect too much out of anyone too soon.

While some people found it "sad" that Grace pretty much ignored Jack and Henry for the first six months, I was elated by it. I didn't have to worry about her attempting to pick them up while I wasn't looking, playing horse with them on the floor, or playing hide and seek, choosing to hide a baby!

In the end, even after reading and following the program outlined in *Parenting Your Strong-Willed Child*, I learned that I could spend twenty-four hours a day playing with Grace and some days, it still wasn't enough, and never would be. That realization was a blessing. It took away some of the guilt I continuously felt, asking myself if I was paying enough attention to her and including her enough, despite the strain placed on my time by having three young children.

At the end of the day, your kids just need to know you love them. They need to feel secure in your home and in your love for them. You do the best you can for all your children and yourself, and then you go to bed!

PRESSURE TO "EDUCATE" YOUR BABIES

Rivers know this: there is no hurry. We shall get there some day.
　　　—*Pooh's Little Instruction Book*, inspired by A.A. Milne

In the beginning, your babies are going to sleep—a lot. Personally, I think they've got the right idea. I have never understood toddlers who throw a tantrum at the mere mention of a nap. I would *kill* to have someone tuck me into my bed every afternoon and say, "Honey, you just sleep as long as you like."

With all the articles and books on the market that emphasize the importance of nurturing your babies' intelligence and the opportunity to create geniuses if only they are stimulated in the "right" way, I believe many women think that means you must begin educating your babies from day one. Nothing could be further from the truth.

The education, for lack of a better word, you need to give your babies now is the knowledge that you will always be there for them. That when they cry, you will pick them up (provided you aren't juggling their sibling). That you will feed them when they are hungry. That your voice will be the one they hear primarily during the day (at least for the first six weeks or so) and through the night. The bond you are creating with your babies simply by feeding, rocking, and singing to them is enough right now.

Don't feel too pressured by the number of products on the market designed to stimulate babies' brains during this time period. For all of you, less is more right now. You do not need to feel that you should read 3.7 books to each child per day or do the Baby Einstein flashcards at least once before lunchtime to ensure the children's admission to the city's best preschool in three years. There will be more than enough time (and products) for stimulation and playtime in the months ahead. And when that point arrives, you'll look back with fond memories at how quiet it was in the early days (and with no memory of how often you were feeding the babies).

THREE

3-6 Months: The Schedule Begins

TOP TEN THOUGHTS DURING THIS PHASE

10. The "I need more time to heal" excuse isn't going to fend off my husband's desire to "have relations" indefinitely.

9. Is she teething? I think she's teething. Maybe not. No, I think she is. Well...

8. *When* will I fit into my pre-pregnancy clothes?

7. I've got to get out of this house!

6. *How* do I get out of this house with two babies?

5. What money will I shop with, if and when I manage to get out?

4. Are they ever going to sleep through the night twice in a row?

3. Four months is too long to go without a haircut.

2. Will I ever catch up with the *Desperate Housewives*?

1. Oh dear, I think they're thinking about crawling.

A SCHEDULE EMERGES

Ever notice that 'What the hell' is always the right decision?
—Marilyn Monroe

The goal of this period—and one that most parents of twins want to achieve as soon as possible—is to get to the babies on a reliable feeding, napping, *and* nighttime schedule. Getting even one baby on a schedule is not easy. Scheduling two or more is even more challenging. The ultimate objective is to get your babies on the *same schedule*. Otherwise, you will have Johnny on a great schedule, and Jimmy on a great schedule, but you will never have more than six seconds to yourself.

Feeding Schedule

Continue to feed your babies every three to four hours. If your feeding schedule is still all over the place, know that as you introduce consistent naptimes, your babies' daytime feeding schedule will slowly find its groove around those naptimes.

Napping Schedule

Mollie, Barb, Holly, Jean, Sonya, and I agree wholeheartedly on at least one step of this schedule-establishment process: during the 3- to 6-month period, it's imperative to get the babies napping in their cribs if they are not already doing so. Not in swings, not in Pack 'n Plays in the middle of the family room with the TV blaring. Definitely not in your arms. Dr. Liberty concurs: "Parents should start their infants sleeping in their own crib/bassinet as soon as possible (especially before four months of age). Infants can get used to sleeping in car seats, swings, or their parents' arms, and it may become a difficult pattern to break." If your babies already nap in their crib or cribs, give yourself a great big pat on the back, and treat yourself to some chocolate ice cream tonight.

At about the three-month mark, your babies may or may not still be sharing a crib. If they are, and one isn't disturbing the other by moving around too much, feel free to let them nap together, as long as you've gotten the "co-bedding approval" from your pediatrician. Most of our group's babies slept in separate cribs by this point because, if they shared a crib, one baby would fall asleep, and the other would invariably start screaming and wake up the sleeping one.

Another issue our group ran into that prompted the babies to sleep in separate cribs by the three-month mark was that one of the babies was a "scooter." In our case, it was Jack. Even though he wasn't officially rolling yet, he was able to scoot around in the crib. We were concerned that he might inadvertently scoot up against Henry's face and we felt concerned that this wasn't safe. We didn't want Henry breathing carbon dioxide because his face was covered by Jack's leg!

When you're ready to move the babies into their own cribs, it may be a good time to separate the babies into their own rooms, if you've chosen to do that. Barb did this and it worked well. Olivia and Kambria still bonded beautifully despite spending their napping and evening hours apart, and Barb and Tim got about 57 percent more sleep than the rest of us during that time period.

We didn't have enough bedrooms to let the boys each have their own, so we explored a few other options. We contemplated putting one baby's crib in the boys' closet. (This isn't nearly as abusive as it sounds. Their closet is a walk-in.) We tried setting up a Pack 'n Play in our bedroom, and had one baby nap in that and the other baby in his crib. If you attempt this approach, try to ensure that the baby who naps in the Pack 'n Play always naps in the Pack 'n Play. It's important for each baby to become familiar with where he is expected to sleep—sort of follows the Pavlov theory of conditioned reflexes. Kristi found great success with this approach in the early months. Each baby could nap as long as he or she pleased because there was no disruption from another, less-than-pleased baby.

I tried this approach, but neither of my boys was too keen on napping in our bedroom in the Pack 'n Play. Finally, I decided that they would have to learn to sleep in the same room in separate cribs, and they did. I soon discovered that if one cried and woke the other, the one who woke up was on the verge of waking anyway. If he was actually in a deep sleep, he didn't wake up when the other cried. Somewhat sadly, Henry cried so much during his first year of his life that in most instances, Jack couldn't sleep if Henry wasn't crying. The wailing became the white noise Jack needed to drift off. We'd pray for Henry to stop crying, and then he would, only to have Jack start three seconds later.

Another issue parents are concerned about—and one that a few in my group experienced—is that of separating the babies out of the crib they occupied together. Will they miss each other? Will they become anxious, wondering where their sibling is? Mine couldn't care less, but Mollie's boys were *none* too pleased when it came time to be independent. Mollie and Gary's solution to this was simple: they put the boys in separate cribs, but pushed them together so the boys could see each other and sense each other's presence. Each night, they would move the cribs further apart until they were at their "final destinations"—one on one wall and the other on the opposing wall. The separation was gradual and the boys handled it just fine.

One important note: if you *know* you are ultimately going to separate your babies into different rooms, do it early on. You would be surprised by how early the babies will become accustomed to each other's presence, especially during nighttime sleeping hours, and will be devastated when deprived of each other's company. Jack and Henry didn't interact during their first eight months of life in a manner that showed a strong emotional connection. But, from four months on, from the minute one was put into his respective crib, if the other wasn't there within ten seconds, the screaming became, well, deafening.

Once you have identified where, at least in the short term, the babies will sleep, it's time to work on the actual napping schedule. After being screamed at by Tommy and Kevin for separating them into their own cribs, Mollie found that they were also not happily getting onto a regular schedule. In an effort to make them (and, in turn, herself) happy, she followed the principles outlined in *Healthy Sleep Habits, Happy Baby*, by Dr. Marc Weissbluth. I highly recommend this book, since it's devoted almost entirely to helping you get your babies on a regular sleeping schedule. In the latest revised version, Dr. Weissbluth includes an entire chapter on twins.

The "sorority" sisters and I suggest working on the morning nap first. An easy rule of thumb is to put the babies down for their morning nap about two hours after they wake up. If you are experiencing life as I did, you're thinking, "Great, one baby gets up at 5:00 a.m. and the other at 6:00 a.m., so I'm already hosed!" Have no fear; this issue is short-lived, if it occurs at all. There will come a time when, unless one baby is significantly more tired than the other (and this will happen occasionally), they will get up at about the same time each morning. Barb's girls—who, remember, have separate bedrooms—still woke up at different times when they were ten months old. However, because Kambria got up around 7:30 a.m., if Olivia wasn't up by 8:00, Barb woke her up so the girls could have breakfast together and start the day on the same schedule. Olivia was none the worse for wear for having been awakened early. (And, I know, you hate Barb already because her girls sleep so late.)

A typical schedule for our group was to feed both babies a bottle when they woke initially, if it was very early. Because my boys got up every morning between five and six o'clock, there was *no* way I was going to do a formal breakfast then. But they would not go back to sleep without something. So, before my husband jumped into the shower, he fed them both a bottle. They'd go back to sleep until seven or eight o'clock. Some of my girlfriends' babies didn't wake up until seven o'clock or later (and yes, I hated them, too—for a while). They simply started the day with breakfast.

Once you've got the morning nap going, work on the afternoon nap (or naps). Obviously, what you can and should expect in terms of scheduled napping will vary, and those expectations will have to be altered as your babies get older. For example, you would not force a baby to adhere to a strict napping schedule when he or she is only three days old. Dr. Weissbluth discusses how long to let a baby cry when waiting (or praying) for them to fall asleep, and how flexible to be with errands and other unscheduled activities in terms of pushing naptimes back or skipping them altogether. In the sorority girls' opinions, Dr. Weissbluth's approach is reasonable; he never professes that, while working to get your babies on a regular schedule, you may never leave the house during common napping hours. I know several people who have successfully used his strategies with twins. Go get the book, feign a headache, sneak up to your bed, and start reading.

Truthfully, the worst part of all this daytime schedule regulation is that, if you have a two-story house, there will come an evening when your husband walks in the door, and you tell him, "Honey, we're moving to a ranch-style home." By then you will feel like you have made at least one thousand trips per day up and down the stairs to take the babies to their napping zones. Try to bear with it. It's good exercise and it will be worth it in the end.

Sample Daily Schedule

Unreasonably early waking	Bottle
8:30ish	Breakfast
9:30ish – 11:30ish	Morning nap
Noon	Bottle
1:30ish	Afternoon nap
5:00	Dinner
*8:00	Bedtime bottle
8:30	Bedtime
*11:00	Bedtime bottle

*Your babies may go to bed successfully at 8:30 p.m. and sleep until 4:00 a.m. or so. Or, you might find that they still need that 11:00 p.m. bottle to make it until 4:00 a.m. or later. This last bottle may end up being given at any point between 8:00 p.m. and midnight, until such a time that the babies (one or the other—or, with any luck, both) don't wake up for it.

These times are complete estimates. When your babies are under six months of age, they will most likely have an early evening nap plugged in to the schedule as well. By the time they are six to eight months old, you'll know when they need to eat and sleep as well as when you can safely run morning errands. When my boys were nine months old, I learned that they could skip the morning nap if I needed to be out and about, and then they would go down earlier in the afternoon.

One word of warning: *do not* assume that because your babies skip the morning nap they will sleep for four hours in the afternoon. I often put my boys down around 12:30 p.m. and thought, "Okay, I've got three hours on my hands. I'll start some major project," only to hear them whimpering two hours later. The good news: if they skip the morning nap and take only a short afternoon nap, you can push their bedtime up and do your project in the evening. For every downside, there is almost always an upside. Keep this perspective and you will have survived the first year before you know it.

Nighttime Schedule

In many cases at this stage, parents could not care less about the daytime feeding and napping schedules as long as they (the parents) are sleeping for six to eight hours straight at night. Therefore, by the time the babies are three months of age, it's not uncommon for parents of newborn twins to search almost frantically for a nighttime sleep training approach that they agree with, and—more importantly— that works.

So many theories have been presented regarding at what age babies can sleep through the night—not to mention misunderstandings regarding what defines "through the night"—that it is often challenging for parents to know where to start. Add to their confusion the probability that parents are exhausted when they begin to research the latest and greatest sleep training approaches, and they quickly feel like they're running in circles with two drops of gas in the tank, while trying to figure out which approach to try any given night.

One key point to remember through the nighttime discussion is that, technically, sleeping through the night means sleeping for six hours straight. I remember when the nurse at my pediatrician's office told me this. Grace was about three months old. I looked at her like she had told me that Christmas had been cancelled for the next seven years.

When I regrouped, I said, "So...you mean...if she falls asleep at 9:00 p.m. and wakes up at 3:00 a.m., she has technically slept through the night?" She answered, "Yes." I think my exact response was "Well, that's crap!" I wanted to grab the medical practitioner who came up with that timetable—undoubtedly a man without children—and get his license revoked. I mean, really, it would have felt better to hear the nurse say, "Okay, Elizabeth, your child is simply not sleeping through the night yet," rather than cause me to question why I look like holy hell. After all, "She's sleeping through the night!"

Hopefully I've saved you the utter disgust you will feel if your own pediatrician had told you this. The truth is, even if your babies fall asleep at 9:00 p.m. and wake at 3:00 a.m., it is oh-so-much easier than when they were waking up every two hours on opposing schedules. You and your husband can switch nights of responsibility or each feed a different baby. So while you may not be out of the "I'm-not-snoozing-through-the-night" woods yet, once your babies are sleeping for six or seven hours straight, you've made a definite step in that direction.

There are two basic approaches to sleep training. The first is to let your babies scream until they fall asleep. This approach is often referred to as "Ferberizing," because it is the approach most strongly supported by Dr. Richard Ferber, a well-known sleep specialist who encourages parents to let their babies "cry it out" while learning to put themselves to sleep on their own. The alternate approach is a gentler one, and it's advocated by the majority of today's sleep-training experts. More often than not, newer approaches do *not* encourage parents to let their babies scream for hours on end, especially at an early age. The newest experts in this area understand—and agree with—the fact that parents want an approach that is firm, but also gentle and kind. The bottom line is, it's important to identify an approach that works for you and your family, and be confident in your decision. It's your choice to make, and it should be based on what you believe will work best in *your* situation.

You must also acknowledge that no matter which approach you choose, it may not work perfectly on night one. Or night two. Most experts' gradual approaches involve multiple steps. Step one may not be successful on night one. Step three may not be successful the first, second, or third time you attempt it. So often, David and I tried a new step (or a new strategy altogether, sure that the previous one wasn't the one by which our children were *ever* going to learn to sleep), and it failed miserably on night one. So the next night we tried something altogether different. This was not the way to go. For one thing, our babies were horribly confused (as were we). For another, it's possible that a particular strategy *is* the right one for you and your babies, but the particular night on which you choose to introduce it *isn't* right. Perhaps one or both of the babies isn't feeling well. Perhaps your babies simply need a few nights to get used to a new routine. If you give any strategy a week or so of consistent use, it will become genuinely clear whether it's the right one or whether you need to go in search of Plan B (or Plan K, as we were on before we had success, given our haphazard approach).

A magnificent book that has come on the market since Jack and Henry were babies is *Good Night, Sleep Tight: The Sleep Lady's Gentle Guide to Helping Your Child Go To Sleep, Stay Asleep, and Wake Up Happy* by Kim West. West's approach is similar to Dr. Weissbluth's in that she does not recommend forcing your baby to cry himself to sleep. Rather, she advocates a gradual approach for parents who feel traumatized by the thought of enforcing a bedtime schedule for children who want to be held or rocked by their parents all night long.

West also provides personal consultations. I know someone who used West for this when her twins were nearly one year old, and were still not sleeping through the night or napping well during the day. Within a week of employing

West's customized strategy, my friend's babies were on a schedule that worked for everyone in that particular family. Find out more about West, her book, and her consultations at http://www.sleeplady.com.

Another popular newcomer is Suzy Giordano. Her book, *Twelve Hours' Sleep by Twelve Weeks Old*, is one of the newest to hit the "we-need-this-baby-to-sleep-now" scene. The title alone offers a guarantee of sorts that not many new parents would turn down. Important to note: Suzy is a mother of twins herself. In 1995, after she established a sleep training approach that worked wonderfully with her own twins, she shared her strategies—which include regular feeding times, regular napping times, and ultimately, the "peace of mind that comes with taking the parent and child out of the anxiety and chaos of a sleep deprived world"—with a friend who had triplets. Giordano's approach indeed worked for the triplets (those must have been two happy parents), and a career was born.

Like Kim West, Giordano offers personal consultations with expectant parents looking to be proactive as well as exhausted parents looking for a miracle. Parents in the Washington, D.C. area have benefited from Suzy's face-to-face consultations for years, and I know a couple who consulted with her and, even better than expected, had *eleven*-week-old twins sleeping for twelve hours at night.

Her consulting rates vary based on the length and breadth of service requested. For more information on Giordano's services available for those living within or outside of the Washington, D.C. metropolitan area, visit her website at http://www.babycoach.net.

While David and I can't come even remotely close to professing ourselves experts on nighttime sleep training, there is one important lesson we learned over the years, through our own trial and error, that we believe should be added to the above experts' recommendations. Once the babies are waking only once per night, don't change their diapers unless they really need new ones. More often than not at this point, they can go up to ten hours or so without a diaper change. Avoiding it will get you back to bed quicker and will not prompt your babies to wake up any more than they already have. They can have the bottle they need and doze off right away. If they don't realize they are awake to begin with, they won't know they are eating in the middle of the night and learn to rely on doing so.

At some point during this phase, you will determine an acceptable bedtime for your babies. It may be as early as 8:30 p.m. or as late as 11:00 p.m. The time will be determined by a variety of things, not the least of which is your babies' gestational age and weight at birth. Work with your pediatrician to determine the bedtime with which you'll have the most success in terms of the number of hours *you* will be able to sleep before a baby needs you. Remember, if your babies go to bed at 6:00 p.m., but awaken at 11:00 and are up every three hours thereafter, the fact that they're sleeping for five hours straight won't mean much to you—especially if you and your husband don't go to bed until 10:00 p.m.

Once you establish the babies' bedtime and are confident that they can go six hours or so without eating, you should have a plan for dealing with those nights when one or both of the babies wakes up before the six-hour mark. The process of sleep-teaching (or "sleep-guiding," as Kim West refers to it— a phrase I love) has two components: helping the babies fall asleep on their own in their beds, and getting them to *stay* asleep until they wake up from real hunger.

If a baby (or two) wakes up and you think, "He cannot *possibly* be hungry," check on him or them to make sure that he isn't stuck in an uncomfortable position or in need of a diaper change. If all is well, quietly reassure him with your voice. *Do not pick him up!* I cannot stress this enough. You are not being cruel. If you feel you must pick up that baby, be prepared for the fact that you will be doing it the next night, and the next, and the next. What the baby is learning is that—barring a true physical need—if he cries loud enough and long enough, you will do what he wants. It's amazing how quickly babies train their parents.

If you'd like, you can follow the example of Jamie and Paul Buckman from *Mad About You*. Sit outside the door and be in "pain" with your child or children. Or, get earplugs. Or, turn up the volume on the TV so high you think the appliance might combust right in front of you. Go downstairs and vacuum. Try something, anything, to keep yourself from giving in. I remember the day I told Mollie I felt so abusive for forcing the boys to cry at night after they'd only been in bed for two hours. I thought they were learning that they could not count on me. She snapped me back to reality as only Mollie can. "Liz," she said, "if they had a real need, you would help them. You always do. That's how they know they can count on you. They need to learn to go to sleep and to put themselves back to sleep when they wake up prematurely. It's a life skill. They don't realize that yet, but you do. You are their mother and you know best. You are rational and logical and they are not. And, by the way, when you do give in, once you leave their room, they lie back in their crib and whisper 'sucker!'"

I nearly died of laughter, but I knew she was right. I worked really hard at it, and within a week or two, both babies slept for ten or eleven hours most nights. I finally had complete confidence that they *could* sleep through the night, so when they woke at midnight, I knew that either something was wrong, or they would go back to sleep if I gave them time. It was easier to convince myself on their "off nights" that I wasn't the most abusive mother on Earth.

STARTING SOLIDS

Never eat more than you can lift.

—Miss Piggy

I'm addressing this topic in the 3-6 Month section even though, most likely, you will not start your babies on solids until they are closer to six months old. If your doctor has not advised you to start solids early for medical reasons, let *me* advise you—*wait!* I know, the thought of doing something new, especially if these are your first babies, is unbearably exciting, however, a week into it, you'll wonder why on earth you decided to start this before you had to. But by that point, the babies will possibly be too used to the new novelty themselves to back up.

Let me elaborate. Today, if you have to go somewhere, you pack bottles. Once you start feeding your babies solid food, you will have to pack said food, spoons, bibs, and possibly a feeding chair of some sort. You will also have to find an easy way to feed them this food in their strollers, car seats, or your lap. Today, when you feed them, you only have to clean their bottles (and potentially change their outfits if they spit up). Once you start solid food, you will have to clean the highchairs, the bibs, the floor, the babies' faces, and maybe even wash their hair since they will likely put their food-covered hands in it and try to accomplish a shampoo job themselves. It's a lot of extra work just for a little excitement and the knowledge that you are doing something new. So, if you are at a point where you feel you *must* have something new in the routine, incorporate a trip to the library once a week or something.

The other reason I mention solid foods in this chapter is so you can prepare yourself. Yes, there is preparation here, too. (Don't worry, by the time this first year is completed, you will be so skilled at being prepared, you will be prepared for being *unprepared!*) For starters, get a jump-start on ensuring that you have the proper equipment for feeding solids. As I mentioned in the section on gear (I believe that repetition is often highly appreciated by mothers of multiples), highchairs are good, but in my experience—and that of my girlfriends—booster-like seats are better. Why?

They don't take up nearly as much room as a highchair because you just strap the booster onto a kitchen chair. Also, they are easily transportable for those times when you will be at someone else's house during a mealtime.

This type of seat typically has two or three different height settings and a three- or four-position recline. The seat can be fully reclined for bottle feedings, and, as the babies gain more strength, you can make the chairs stand up straighter. Better yet, the entire product is dishwasher safe. If you can fit the whole thing in your dishwasher, it'll get it as clean as new after it gets so dirty that you are embarrassed to take it anywhere.

You will need to decide whether to buy commercially prepared baby food or make your own. Now, like breastfeeding versus bottle-feeding, this decision is entirely up to you. I have no issue whatsoever with commercially prepared baby food—except for the price and, at times, the variety offered. Knowing what we spent per week for our daughter to eat commercially prepared baby food, we estimated that we would spend approximately $300 per month to feed the boys. Gives you real insight into how quickly forty-seven-cent items can add up! In addition, there are so many of us with twins living within a two-mile radius of each other that we knew we would have to strategically schedule our baby-food trips to the grocery store so that we didn't buy them out before the next one of us had a chance to shop.

I grimaced initially at the thought of making my own baby food. It sounded like a lot of work that would require a tremendous amount of time—something I was short on to begin with. My neighbor, Krisi, was making baby food for her son and insisted it was the easiest process on earth. I decided to give it a try, and she was right. It's incredibly easy and doesn't take nearly as much time as you might imagine. You simply have to be efficient about it (and at this point, you're bound to be a world-class expert on efficiency).

The first thing to do if you want to go this route is get a food mill—and not one of the mini food mills sold at baby stores. You need a *real* food mill. Plus, when you've finished making baby food with it, you can use it to make pasta sauces from the tomatoes you grow in your garden—you know, in your spare time. The only other necessities are a food processor, a steamer basket, freezer bags, and ice trays—preferably the kind with angled cubes so you can stack the trays without sinking one tray's cubes into those of the tray below it.

Barb thought I was nuts when I started making my own baby food. She gave it a try one day—I think mainly in an effort to prove that I was indeed nuts—and within three weeks she was hooked. Of our entire group, I think only Jean and Sonya didn't turn themselves into baby-food chefs once a week. They were happy as clams running to the grocery, loading their carts with baby food jars, and calling it a day. And, therefore, they should by all means have continued to do just that.

These days, there are a myriad of quality websites devoted to making baby food. There is an endless array of recipes and helpful hints available. One of my favorite sites is http://www.wholesomebabyfood.com, but if you do a Google search on 'homemade baby food,' you will be greeted by pages and pages of sites with baby-food-making directions, recipes, safety tips, etc.

There are also many wonderful books on the market devoted entirely to making your own baby food. Ruth Yaron's *Super Baby Food* is the most comprehensive I have seen. It details options for making baby food from their first bite through the toddler years and beyond. A mother of twins herself, Ruth provides an enormous amount of information on why homemade baby food can be more beneficial (not to mention easier and less expensive) than its commercially prepared counterpart—and provides unmatchable variety at the same time. (Even I grew tired of graham crackers and goldfish crackers, and I wasn't even the one eating them!)

Additionally, throughout her book, Ruth addresses such challenges as the "picky eater" and the "seemingly endless eater," and even includes a month-by-month schedule for the introduction of foods in the first year (which offers *far* more dietary options than commercially prepared baby food). If there are any foods suggested that make you uncomfortable, either skip them or call your pediatrician to obtain their advice.

If anything, during this three- to six-month period, you might start your babies on cereal if advised by your doctor to do so. Most babies start with rice cereal and then move to oatmeal and barley. I started with rice, but Henry was so constipated that even after starting him on prunes before cereal so that we could mix it with the cereal, he wasn't able to process it. We moved him (and hence, Jack as well) to oatmeal. (You want to see me crazy? Have me make one bowl of oatmeal and one bowl of rice cereal twice a day *and* remember who is supposed to get which.)

The best approach, as long as one of your babies is not sick, is to make one or two bowls of cereal or other food, get one spoon, and go back and forth from mouth to mouth. And in all honesty, if one kid is sick, he's probably already passed the germs to the other, but to make myself feel like a decent, caring mother, I used separate bowls and spoons if one or both of the boys was obviously under the weather.

In the beginning, it's easiest to feed one baby his cereal at breakfast time and feed the other baby after the first has finished, or feed the other baby cereal for lunch or dinner. While they are learning to eat from a spoon, it will be difficult to feed them both in the same sitting. And if you have two bowls, well, forget it. You'll be putting one bowl down to get the other bowl and both babies will be protesting—one because he sees you feeding his sister and the other because she has a mouthful of food and doesn't know what to do with it!

When introducing new foods, make sure that you feed the babies the new food for four or five days before adding an additional menu item. Once you know that the babies can tolerate a particular food, you can combine it with a new one, because if they have a reaction, you know it is the newest food that has caused it. I tried to keep my boys on the same schedule with new foods. However, Henry had prunes before Jack (due to the constipation issues), and just to be sure I didn't forget who had tried what, I kept a sticky note on the inside of my cabinet that listed which foods each baby had successfully tried.

WHAT'S GOING ON NOW?

You need chaos in your soul to give birth to a dancing star.
—Friedrich Wilhelm Nietzsche

Another day, another new development. During the first year, so many new things will occur that there will be days when you don't know whether to think, "Hey, this is cool, something new!" or "Good Lord, could we *please* get some semblance of a stable routine in this house?" There are more than a few developmental milestones that could emerge, or begin to emerge, during this three- to six-month period.

Important Points to Keep in Mind

Respect the "Guidelines"
The guidelines provided by infant development experts are just that—guidelines. If your babies are not following the "standard" pattern of development, do not panic. Close the book that proclaims that your child should be doing cartwheels by nine months of age and place a call to your pediatrician (during normal business hours). There are many full-term babies who do not follow the standard pattern of

development and even more premature babies who do not.

There is a Wide Range of "Normal"

There is a wide range of within-normal-limits for any developmental milestone. Your friend's babies might reach a milestone at the early end of the range while your babies might accomplish it at the later end, but they are both developing on track.

Don't Compare

Try as hard as possible not to compare your babies' development to that of your friends' babies, whether they, too, are multiples, or whether they are singletons. All babies are different and they are going to develop at their own pace. You may find that your friend's baby is rolling over at seven months of age and yours is not. However, do a little more talking and you may learn that your baby says, "Mama," while your friend's baby doesn't even seem to know who "Mama" is!

Be Patient

Babies develop new skills quickly and usually at the most embarrassing time. My girlfriend Sonya had taken her boys to the doctor for their nine-month appointment and swore up, down, left, right, and center that her boys made little effort to get from point A to point B. As she was explaining this, the doctor started laughing, and Sonya turned to see one of her sons using his heels to go backward on the table.

Similarly, Mollie was concerned because at nine months, her boys would not sit unassisted to save themselves. The doctor told her that if they were still not sitting at ten and a half months, they would discuss a plan of action. Two days later, the boys were sitting unassisted for thirty minutes at a time. The lesson is: don't fear that because your babies are not doing something today, it means that they still won't have mastered it two weeks from now. They gain both motivation and, in turn, skills quickly.

TEETHING

If you were to open up a baby's head—and I am not for a moment suggesting that you should—you would find nothing but an enormous drool gland.

—Dave Barry

Every time my daughter cried—practically from the moment she was born until she had a mouth full of teeth—people proclaimed, "Oh, she must be teething." They also believed this to be true because she drooled like crazy from the moment she was born. The same thing happened with Jack and Henry. They cried and drooled and drooled and cried, and everyone said that, surely, they were teething.

I know that teeth bother babies long before anyone actually sees those pearly whites. They cause discomfort as they ascend through the gums. Somehow, however, I doubt it took eight months for them to make their full ascent, but I'm not a dentist. Barb, however, is a dental hygienist, and I called her probably sixteen times too many asking (as if she had a crystal ball handy), "Well, today it looks like thus and such. Do you think he'll get the tooth today?" Her answer was typically, "Maybe. Maybe not." And she was always right.

Honestly, just when you finally have some sense of a schedule, and your babies have slept for eleven hours straight for, say, two nights, they will suddenly regress—because they really are teething! They will wake up crying and/or will not go to bed easily. They may cry while drinking their bottles. Don't worry, it's just the universe keeping you on your toes and making sure you don't get too comfortable. After all, you are not allowed to do that until they turn one, remember?

Most of us were sure that our babies' teeth were coming up a little and then going back down *over* and *over* until they finally came in—only to have the peace interrupted for the next tooth that decided, that day, to begin its trek to daylight.

During the day, Kristi kept a Ziploc bag of teething toys in the refrigerator. After meals, when her twins were still in their highchairs, she offered each of them two to choose from. These were also available when they appeared to have trouble with their teeth at other times throughout the day.

Tylenol works wonders for teething, especially right before bedtime, which is when most babies seem to be bothered most by the discomfort. Many parents don't like to share the droppers that come with infant Tylenol between babies, just in case they are sick. Kristi's solution: one bottle got a round green sticker on the front with the first letter of one child's name written on it, and the other got a round red sticker with the first letter of the other child's name written on it. This way, each child always got medicine from his or her own bottle.

Many pediatricians do not recommend using topical anesthetics to relieve teething pain, but Barb swore by using just the slightest bit of baby Orajel right before bedtime. Her girls' teeth didn't bother them enough to wake them during the night, but they did bother them enough to prevent them from falling asleep. The Orajel took the edge off enough that they could drift off. I was always paranoid about overmedicating my boys, but after a while, I learned what behavior was normal and what was "off." When it's off, all parents develop a bit of a sixth sense when it truly is their teeth (especially after that first one comes in and you can say with confidence that your child actually has teeth under his gums somewhere).

GET ME OUT OF THIS HOUSE!

The more things change, the more they remain...insane.
—Michael Fry and T. Lewis, *Over the Hedge*

One morning during the three- to six-month period, you are going to wake up and say, "I have *got* to get out of this house." Your comfort with the babies' immune systems will be higher, and if not, your lack of comfort staring at your walls will propel you to call the pediatrician and beg him or her to tell you that it is fine for you all to run to the mall, the bank, or the park.

The best description for a first outing is: simple. Choose a location from which you can leave in a hurry if you have to (not the grocery store when you are trying to buy a week's worth of groceries). My first outing was to the mall (remember that early-on proclamation that I would *never* take all three kids shopping?). I had all three kids and it went beautifully—or maybe I just have selective memory. Try to time your babies' bottles simultaneously and leave directly after they eat so you have a few hours. Because you are trying to get them on a schedule as well, this is the perfect opportunity to get out and put them in the position where they cannot sleep or eat for a while (though usually at this age, if they really need it, they can still sleep fairly well in the stroller). If they are awake, they will likely be distracted enough by the unfamiliar scenery that they won't have time to think they are hungry. As time goes by, work your way up the errand ladder. Within a couple of months, Barb could successfully complete about six brief errands in a row with her girls (not including a trip to the grocery store for a week's worth of groceries).

Solutions to Getting Out and About

Grocery Store

While your babies are still in infant carriers, put one in his carrier in the cart's front seat and one in the big part of the cart. If you are not getting too many things, you can probably fit groceries around the kid in the bigger part of the cart. If you are getting a lot of things, do what Mollie did and pull another cart behind you. I am, unfortunately, not coordinated enough for this option.

Another idea is to put one baby in his car seat in the cart's front seat and carry the other baby in a front-pack carrier. This allows you all the room of the cart for groceries. Should you have a toddler with you as well, you might try one of those fun little carts with the car in front. When we tried this approach, Grace rode in the car part, one baby stayed in his car seat in the front of the cart, and I carried the other baby in a front-pack carrier. It should be noted that I did this only once and I was in a full sweat when I was finished (I think it was February in Chicago). I put everyone in their places, went full steam ahead, and assumed the talk-to-the-hand stance each time a fellow shopper began to approach with her soon-to-be-asked question written all over her face. But I got all my groceries purchased.

As soon as the babies get older and are no longer in their infant car seats, you can sit one in the cart's front seat, put the other either in a front-pack carrier (if you can still carry her that way), or put her in a baby backpack. Sonya did this and said that it worked wonderfully. Some forward-thinking establishments actually have carts with tandem front seats. I have become a very loyal patron of those establishments.

Key to your success: make sure all the grocery necessities are at the top of the list and shop for those first. Once you've gotten those, if all is still going well, move on to the other items on the list.

Warehouse Clubs

Put the babies in their stroller (a side-by-side stroller is undoubtedly not going to work for this excursion) and pull a cart behind you. Another option I discovered when I got to one such store and realized I did not have my stroller in the trunk—sit both babies together (minus infant car seats) in the cart's front seat. Now, pay attention. You put their backs to the sides of the seat and put the right foot of the baby on your left through the slot and the left foot of the baby on your right through the slot. Their opposing legs just bend up next to each other in the seat.

This approach did not work too well for me until the boys were about ten months old and were sitting up extremely well, and it only works for about thirty minutes at a time, but necessity is the mother of invention and this was my invention on that particular day.

Target (and Other Quick Stops)

These are the perfect places to shop with your babies in their stroller. Lots of times, you are only browsing or picking up an item or two, which you can easily carry while pushing your stroller with your other hand (or place in your stroller's storage basket). If you will be buying a lot of items, pull a cart behind you. Or, try putting both babies in the front seat of the cart if they are strong enough, and use the bigger part of the cart to hold your purchases.

The Mall

The stroller is definitely your best bet here. A recommendation: have a front-back double stroller for this trip. I tried using my double jogging stroller for about six months after which I finally decided I was tired of not being able to get through Baby Gap with any ease whatsoever. Once, I got stuck—truly stuck—in Ann Taylor between rounders of clothes. An employee had to come and rescue me by relocating the rounders (as well as the racks around them). She didn't seem to find my predicament the least bit amusing; clearly she had not yet had children. After that, I broke down and bought the front-back double stroller. Again, it was the best purchase I have made since the boys were born.

As for family dinner outings, the time period when the babies are still in their infant car seats is a great one for taking them to a local, family-friendly restaurant. If you are worried about the mass of people and germs, you are not alone.

Choose a restaurant where you order at a counter and then pick your table. The crowd at this type of establishment is often minimal (especially early in the evening), as is the noise level. You and your spouse can eat at your own pace and leave when you need to.

If you have a toddler in tow, be prepared for the fact that the dinner may be a bit more chaotic than it might be if you didn't. There were times when Grace was, for lack of better terminology, a holy terror the minute we entered the restaurant. But there were other times when Grace was a perfect angel and, after the boys screamed their way through dinner, David and I requested to-go containers and took our food home.

At times during this first year, David and I were too tired to justify the cost and hectic nature of going out to dinner with infant twins and a two-year-old. And other times, the joy of being out—especially on the first gorgeous spring evening—was worth every one of the acrobatics required to get us through the meal. One of our favorite restaurants when the kids were all under the age of three was a local grill. The kids all shared a pasta dish, and David and I were often actually able to finish our meals (though we suffered from major heartburn afterward because, sure that someone would have a meal-ending meltdown any second, we ate far too quickly).

As the babies get older, they will enjoy more and more simply watching all the people around them. And the people around them will be so enthralled with them (as you have undoubtedly already learned) that they will make faces at them and otherwise entertain them while you eat. Yes, you may have to address those fellow diners who think your babies are public property and come over to touch them, but in the grand scheme of things, it's worth it to get out for a few hours.

Another option, if the weather is cooperative, is to pack a picnic and head to a local park or other nice spot. The point is to get out and spend some time together as a family.

A WAIST IS A TERRIBLE THING TO MIND

The specific story line that people have responded to the most has been the horror of bathing suit shopping.

—Cathy Guisewite

I remember my obstetrician coming into my recovery room at the hospital to give me my discharge instructions. After I got a huge laugh out of the "no intercourse for six weeks" segment of his lecture, I got serious when he mentioned that most women who give birth to twins come to their six-week appointment weighing less than they did before they got pregnant. As I stared down at my still seven-month-pregnant-looking stomach, I thought, "Could that be true?"

In fact, no. It's not true. I mean, it may be true for some women who have the metabolism of a two-year-old, but for the general population, I do not believe it is true. And frankly, the women for whom it is are not my friends. It makes me frantic just to look at them. So, when I went in for that six-week appointment, having lost only twenty pounds (which I was sure I had lost in the delivery room), I was dumbfounded and confused.

Here's the bottom line: it took you nearly nine months to put the weight on, and it will take you at least that long to take it off. But, you *will* take it off. I remember commenting to my mom one day that I really needed to exercise because my cholesterol was higher than it should have been, and she said, "Liz, I think you get plenty of exercise. It may not be for thirty minutes straight, but it's there." And she was right.

Think about all the time you spend going up and down stairs, carrying between six and forty-five pounds (During the first year, there were days when I didn't feel like going up the steps more than once, and therefore, simply carried both boys. Toward the end of that year, they each weighed twenty-three pounds.) You constantly get up and down out of chairs, you bend over and pick up babies, you shake bottles, you clean up spots and spills off the floor… Need I go on? This is all exercise!

When the boys were about ten months old, we put our house on the market, and I felt a bit ill one afternoon as I shuttled everyone to the car to accommodate another showing. David asked what I had eaten recently. Using my short-term memory, I told him, about six cupcakes and three or four Cokes. Maybe a piece of bread. That kind of limited food consumption—regardless of the number of empty calories—doesn't breed weight gain, but unfortunately, it doesn't breed energy or good health either. Because both are highly valuable, try to eat high-energy, nutritious foods. If you're finding time to eat three solid, nutritious meals a day, you're my hero.

There are certain types of food that work best for new moms of twins: foods that can be eaten with one hand. Sliced turkey, cheese, and fruit are some of my favorites. And, be *sure* you take a multi-vitamin each day. Ask your doctor which brand he or she recommends.

During that first year, I wanted to eat better all along, but truthfully, most afternoons I was so tired by five o'clock that I didn't have it in me to cook a nice meal. Also, by the time David got home, it was too *late*.

As for a workout routine, if you feel you need one, do what makes you feel good. Barb was on the elliptical machine (I still don't know what one of those looks like) every morning at six thirty once her girls hit four months. I wanted to kill her. Mollie signed up at the YMCA when her boys were nine months old and put them in their nursery while she did aerobics or the treadmill. I'm still rationalizing that the exercise I get going up and down the stairs is adequate, because I hate formal exercise.

While you *will* lose weight, your body will more than likely never be the same. I can now fit into all my old clothes, but I will never, *ever* don a bikini again. I seem to have grown some extra skin on my belly that won't go away. Some call it their "twin skin." I call it my "war flab." Mollie calls it her "duffel bag" that will be forever with her.

While we would all love it to vanish, it provides a memory of those months we spent carrying the babies (small consolation, I know). Now, some say a tummy tuck is the way to go. Maybe. But I don't have $4,000 sitting around, and I don't have three weeks to lie in bed and recover. Therefore, I have resigned myself to the "no bikini" rule and called it a day on the tummy issues.

One little secret from this group: low-rise jeans and pants. I had hips prior to getting pregnant, so you can imagine those hips after carrying and delivering nearly twelve pounds of babies. I would have been the first to insist that *no way* would you ever catch me in low-rise *anything*! But someone dared me to try it, just for the heck of it, and I always had trouble refusing a good dare. I still remember looking in that dressing mirror and staring at myself in disbelief. I hesitantly turned around and looked at my backside. I repeated that exercise about ten times just to be sure I wasn't so tired that I was hallucinating. My final conclusion: they really do work!

Now, let me clarify that I am not talking about the *ultra-low-rise* pants. Those don't work on anyone who wears more than size zero, and most certainly not on someone who has been recently pregnant. The basic low-rise pants are sufficient. They make your rear look smaller, your hips *feel* smaller, and your body feel altogether thinner. Why? Because that "war flab" no longer hangs over the waistband like a ball of dough waiting to be kneaded! An added benefit: several of my friends believe low-rise jeans are a godsend if you delivered by Cesarean section, because they don't rub as uncomfortably on the scar as their higher-rise counterparts.

Another secret: resale shops. Okay, don't go crazy. I am not suggesting you go to resale shops where everything is a mess, and you're lucky if you find pants without six holes and two major stains. As I discovered, there are unbelievably nice resale shops. We have one nearby that specializes in high-end merchandise in fantastic shape. All clothing they buy (and then resell) must arrive cleaned, pressed, and on a hanger. If there is so much as a smudge or an area that looks like it *might* tear, they won't accept it.

I found this particular store to be invaluable during those months when I was "shrinking," but not yet into my pre-pregnancy clothes. It made no sense to go out and buy new clothes at that point—I hoped I would be too big for them in six weeks—but yet, my self-esteem took a beating when I was still wearing maternity clothes at the point the boys were four months old. I found some unbelievable deals (I mean, five dollars for a pair of J. Crew jeans in like-new condition—low-rise, of course!). I continue to shop there today, especially when I have an event for which I have nothing appropriate to wear. I know the next time I have an opportunity to wear such an outfit, it's likely to be long out of style.

So now, I dare *you*. Check out low-rise pants and upscale resale shops in your area that carry clothing for adults. You'll be thrilled with what you find!

CHILDPROOFING

Electricity can be dangerous. My nephew tried to stick a penny into a plug. Whoever said a penny doesn't go far didn't see him shoot across that floor. I told him he was grounded.

—Tim Allen

You are probably saying to yourself, "Childproofing? My babies aren't even rolling over. Why would I need to childproof now?" Well, my friend, your babies will be rolling over before you know it, and, at that point, you will be too busy chasing them to have time to childproof. Here are some easy things to do quickly to provide *basic* childproofing. The rest you can do as you see the need, depending on your children's desires to explore things that should be off-limits. Here goes:

Early Basics

- Put outlet plugs in all outlets.

- Remove all doorstoppers that are the two-piece coil with a rubber bumper on the end. Babies are notorious for taking off that rubber piece and choking on it.

- Purchase a fireplace bumper pad if you have a raised fireplace hearth. Because no one has designed a fancy, aesthetically pleasing bumper pad, don't feel the need to put it up until at least one of the babies is heading for the hearth. It's better to have it around for that day, however, just so you are prepared.

  On the off-chance that your babies do what Jack did and just crawl over and peel the thing off the fireplace every chance they get, I recommend a gate that can be assembled in a variety of shapes, such as a circle or arc. They are often called Supergates or Superyards, and prevent admission to the entire fireplace area.

- Get all cords off the floor. This will probably mean removing lamps from end tables and possibly moving floor lamps. Non-electrical wire, such as speaker wire, can be threaded under the carpet, but electrical wire cannot.

- Put cabinet locks on all lower cabinets, especially in bathrooms. If medicine is stored there, get a tackle box, put the medicine in it, and lock the box with a combination lock. You can never be too safe about keeping medication out of children's reach. As a side note, I did leave one cabinet in the kitchen unlocked and stored all my Tupperware in it. It gave the babies access to one cabinet so they didn't feel utterly and completely restricted, and the Tupperware often entertained them for up to an hour or so.

You may choose to actually put a *lock* on this cabinet if your babies are like Barb's girls. They enjoyed the Tupperware so much that they'd get it out and push it back and forth across the hardwood floor, making a horribly high-pitched noise like running one's fingernails down a chalkboard. In the process, this game began to destroy her hardwood.

As my boys approached thirteen months, I, too, considered locking the cabinet, as their favorite pastime was letting one crawl inside the cabinet while the other closed the door on him, relegating him to total darkness until he screamed so loud that his relatives in Nebraska could hear him.

Next Level of Childproofing

You will need to do the following once you see the "I'm-going-to-start-moving-soon" twinkle in your babies' eyes:

- Install gates at the top and bottom of your stairs. Also handy are gates used to keep the babies in a particular room to play as you clean adjacent rooms, cook, or are otherwise occupied without worrying where they are or what they are into.

- Research toilet locks. I discovered the beauty of toilet locks the day I found Jack splashing about in our toilet. It took him about eight seconds to get in there while I was changing Henry's diaper.

I have been told by other moms who've tried them that toilet locks have a tendency not to come off easily or completely when you are finished with them, so at a minimum, get into the habit of keeping your toilet lids down and the bathroom doors closed.

- Research oven locks. Believe me, it doesn't matter how tall your children are. Once they realize that the oven door can open, they will try to open it. One day I found Jack and Henry working together to pull the oven door open. (One of them had moved a stool over to it just to get a little extra help in the height department, and if I recall correctly, they both had one foot on the stool.)

  There are several products on the market to keep your oven door safely closed (and keep the knobs from being operational by anyone except an adult). If you do a Google search on "oven safety locks," you will be presented with multiple sites that sell them. There are different styles: one affixes to the side and front of your oven and you unlock it when you need to pull the oven door open. This type of lock won't work if your oven is wedged tightly between cabinets. Thankfully, Safety 1st came out with a product designed for that type of oven-cabinet configuration. It's called the Oven Front Lock, and it fits all ovens including built-ins.

  If your children are as strong and/or resourceful as mine were, they may figure out how to rip any lock off. I became convinced that I could super glue locks onto things, and Jack and Henry would still figure out how to get them loose. If all else fails, do what Mollie did. I went into her house one day and about fell over. She had the thing duct taped. She said it was the saddest thing ever because she doesn't even *use* her oven. In fact, Gary (her husband) usually hides her Christmas presents in there, because he says it's the last place she's likely to look!

ROLLING OVER

Cocooned inside our private dramas we often don't realize life is rolling by us like it should.

—Waiter Rant

The sight of one or both of your babies rolling over is your first indication that times are a-changin'. It is so exciting to see one of your babies roll over for the first time. Pretty soon, he'll start on one end of the room and end up at the other end just by rolling his way across to get to something. So when you see it happening, grab the video camera—and then be prepared to keep shooting that baby lying flat on her back because all babies know when they are expected to perform and are rarely willing to comply.

FOUR

6-12 Months: You're Halfway There!

TOP TEN PRAYERS FOR THIS PHASE

10. When you turn one year old, please weigh at least twenty pounds so we can turn these car seats around.

9. Please grant me one adult conversation per day.

8. Please provide me with a new and exciting indoor activity to do tomorrow. It's winter and it's freezing.

7. Please let my hairdresser have an opening soon. I barely recognize myself!

6. Please make all that crying part of a dream. Keep trying.

5. Please let there be clean clothes in the closet and edible food in the refrigerator when I wake up in the morning.

4. Let the person on the other end of that ringing phone be calling to tell me that, despite the chaos in this house at this moment, I'm the most wonderful, talented mother in the entire world!

3. Please keep the food *on* the tray!

2. Please help these children understand that if they don't heed my gentle "No," they will be forcibly removed from the hearth. And please help them not to have a raging fit when that occurs.

1. It's 3:00 in the morning. If there is a God in heaven, please help that baby understand (and soon) that he is *not hungry*!

Great news—you're halfway there! Even better news—the toughest half is behind you. I promise the next six months will go by so quickly, you will hardly believe it. Of course, you will still have challenges. And you will be constantly developing and refining strategies for dealing with them, but you will feel oh-so-much more capable. For starters, you will be operating (most of the time) with a good night's sleep! You'll also be more comfortable with your babies' flexibility, schedules, and personalities. You'll know what you can get away with, and what you cannot.

By this point, your babies should be on a fairly set schedule. It's likely to change just a tad over the next six months as the babies give up (every so often) their morning naps, further define when and how much they will eat, and transition almost entirely to table foods.

If you're still fighting the pounds you put on during your pregnancy, this is when you'll shed them. The reason? You're moving constantly. Why? Because your babies are moving constantly. During this six-month period, they are learning to crawl, and start cruising around furniture. If you're really being put to the test, they start walking.

At eleven months, Jack was ready for the Boston Marathon, but Henry wasn't even crawling. The pediatrician had Henry continue physical therapy once a week, but I decided that not only would he do it when he was ready, but the universe was looking out for me. To have two children moving as fast as Jack was moving would put me in a constant sweat.

During this period, you will definitely want to acquire gates and set boundaries for your babies: what they are allowed and not allowed to play with, in, on, or under.

WHAT PART OF "NO" IS UNCLEAR?

If the person you are talking to doesn't appear to be listening, be patient. It may simply be that he has a small piece of fluff in his ear.
—*Pooh's Little Instruction Book*, inspired by A. A. Milne

Your babies start to understand the word "No" during this time frame. Whether they obey it or not is another story. Jack absolutely understood what "No" meant early on. One time, as he attempted to scale the fireplace, I calmly said, "Jack, no no." He slowly turned his head, looked at me, gave me a mischievous smile, turned back, and continued what he was doing. It was as though he wanted to see how many times I'd say "No" before I got up and dragged myself to the other side of the room to move him (which only kept him away from that fireplace for about twenty seconds).

It's important that your children understand "No," but it's equally important that they not hear it all the time. They'll start to wonder what they *can* explore, and the word "No" loses its meaning if used too often.

Remove those things in your home that pose an unsafe distraction to your babies. Use "No" when necessary to keep them from climbing on fireplaces, pulling over chairs, or attempting to play with outlets (even though they are covered). But it's also important not to make your home resemble a padded box. Your babies need to learn to respect boundaries.

Otherwise, when you go to a friend's house—one who has all her beautiful Lladros on prominent display—and you say, "No" to your child as he's getting ready to grab the biggest and most expensive one, he won't understand what you're saying (or potentially that you are talking to *him*), and you'll find yourself the proud owner of a (broken) Lladro.

We had a whole room designated as the toy room. It was technically a dining room, but we didn't have the time or energy to entertain more than this family, so we converted it into the toy room. Nothing in there was off limits for the babies. I could gate them in or put them there to play and not worry. They could safely explore, and I was free from constant in-their-face supervision. They could develop their independence by playing alone or with each other, and I could cook dinner or straighten up the rest of the downstairs (a temporary thing, I assure you).

One suggestion my pediatrician made was to use time-outs when the boys wouldn't obey the word "No." I never found that time-outs worked particularly well with our daughter, but one day Barb called and said she was giving them a go with Olivia and Kambria, so I decided to join her. I didn't want one of my girlfriends to go through any part of this alone!

Our big struggle, and the one I used time-outs for most often, was the TV. The boys were obsessed with it. They pushed all the buttons, turned it on and off, and/or turned the volume up as high as it would go (undoubtedly so they could make a case for the fact that they couldn't hear me as I said, "No").

It drove Grace crazy because the TV continued to flip from *Sesame Street* to the devotional channel, to blaring static, but never back to *Sesame Street*. It drove *me* crazy because they weren't listening to my simple request not to play with the TV. Playing with the television was virtually the only in-house activity to which I said "No" at that point. Everything else was either locked shut, put away, or out of reach.

The boys had hundreds of toys to entertain themselves with and I argued that most of them were far more interesting than a television, but what do I know? Clearly, a thirty-year-old's definition of fun differs a wee bit from that of a pair of one-year-olds.

My first approach was to copy Mollie's self-devised solution to the TV problem. She had Gary go to Home Depot and buy a piece of pre-cut Plexiglas (with rounded edges) the size of their TV control panel. They attached the Plexiglas to the control panel area with Velcro.

Rather ingenious! I didn't have Plexiglas and I needed a solution immediately, so I cut some cardboard and affixed *it* to the TV with Velcro. Within seconds, the boys were ripping it off. Super. Glad I provided them with something to do together, as a team, that didn't involve wrestling or biting. But I quickly got over my joy.

From that point on, each time one of the boys played with the TV, I said, "Please don't play with the TV." They usually looked at me and smiled, but didn't move. Then I said, "Please don't play with the TV, or you'll have to go to time-out." They smiled and continued to play with the TV. To time-out they went. I set up a Pack 'n Play in our dining room (our empty dining room). There were no toys in the room, nothing in the Pack 'n Play, and once in it, the kid couldn't see anyone else in the house unless someone walked past the room.

I usually left them there for just one minute or so. (The times they ended up there together were interesting.) It took many trips to the Pack 'n Play, but after a while they got it. Jack got it more slowly than Henry, but he got it nonetheless. There were still days when they "forgot" the no-TV rule, but it took far fewer trips to the designated time-out zone before they remembered and found another entertaining thing to do.

Barb took another approach for time-outs. She carted each of her girls to a time-out zone upstairs every time one did something she wasn't allowed to do. Truth be told: the time-out zone was the girl's crib. I remember discussing this with her. I said, "Now Barb, all these books say that you shouldn't use a kid's crib for a time-out spot because if you do, she'll see her bed as a 'bad' place and won't want to sleep there!" Barb replied, "I don't care. If I put them in an unconfined spot, they crawl out of it immediately. If I put them in a Pack 'n Play downstairs, they scream at me. I need a break from the screaming. I need. A little. Peace. I'm putting them in time-out in their cribs, and they're going to continue to sleep just fine at night. Period."

It was hard to argue with *that!* I know Barb was making a lot of trips upstairs to her girls' cribs each day. As I've mentioned, Barb is in incredible shape. Despite moving all day long, I am not. Or maybe I just hate heavy breathing and sweat. Either way, I refused to go up and down those steps over and over again each time I used the time-out zone. Besides, for quite a while, each time Jack got out of the time-out zone, he inevitably went right back to doing what got him there in the first place, and therefore had to go back (a good reason not to designate the time-out spot upstairs).

As children get older (past their first birthday), many parents wonder if time-outs are—and have been up until that point—a waste of time. Despite Jo Frost's successes on *Super Nanny,* the reality is that, many times when children are put into a time-out spot, they don't understand why, and the consequence of being there doesn't keep them from pursuing offending behavior right after being "let out."

Until age one, children cannot reason well enough to

understand, "If I do this, this will happen." They don't understand logical or natural consequences for their actions. It may appear they do, because after the ninety-first time, they stop doing it, but it's possible they just got bored and moved on to something else.

While not necessarily the most effective approach to stop less-than-acceptable behavior, a time-out (whether you call it that or not) can be helpful if your child engages in a dangerous activity while you're busy with something else. If you're cooking dinner and your child tries to climb on a chair, throw the television remote, or bite a sibling, it makes sense to put him somewhere—such as a Pack 'n Play—for a short time so you can finish what you are doing and be confident he won't hurt himself or someone else in the meantime.

When babies are able to understand (and respect) their limits a bit more, there are a whole slew of positive approaches to curb undesirable behavior and reinforce positive choices. I talk about these options a lot in my second book, *Ready or Not...There We Go! The REAL Experts' Guide to the Toddler Years with Twins.*

If you'd like to get a bit of information under your belt now (rather than in a year, when you're in the thick of it and can't turn your head for a second to pick up a book), I highly recommend *How to Talk So Kids Will Listen and Listen So Kids Will Talk* by Adele Faber and Elaine Mazlish, as well as *Parent Talk* by Chick Moorman. It may feel foolish reading about negotiating with a child when she has between zero and three words in her repertoire, but employing or at least studying the strategies early on ensures that they escape your mouth more naturally when you really need them! And while the approaches may not be understood by your child when she's less than a year old, there's nothing harmful about using them to promote a positive atmosphere while communicating what's okay and what's not okay.

MODIFYING THE MENU

Variety is the soul of pleasure.

—Aphra Behn

During this period, you go from feeding baby foods (commercially prepared or homemade) to feeding more and more table foods. This is a good thing and a messy thing. I was so excited for the days when my boys could eat finger foods *by themselves*. However, I quickly learned that, although you may have that fifteen-minute break while they're eating, you lose fifteen (sometimes twenty) minutes as you clean up the floor, the trays, and the babies. So, you can take the time to spoon-feed them forever and keep the dining area and the kids clean, or you can let them have at it and just pencil "cleanup time" into your mental daily schedule.

Many moms struggle over which foods to introduce during this period. Obviously, you start with easy-to-pick-up, easy-to-chew, easy-to-swallow foods. You then get bored by them (and so do the babies). When your children are approximately eleven months old, you'll call everyone you know with a small child to ask what on earth they feed them, because you feel positively abusive continuing to give them Cream of Wheat every morning and afternoon.

Some good foods to introduce during this period, when you feel your babies are ready, are:

- Cheerios
- Pieces of bread
- Diced peaches/pears
- Soft green beans
- Black beans
- Pasta
- Soft cereal bars, such as Nutri-Grain bars (broken up)

For additional options, refer to Ruth Yaron's *Super Baby*

Food. Be prepared: picking up this food and putting it into their mouths will take a bit of time. Jack went right at it, hand over fist, but Henry wouldn't touch finger foods for weeks. Once he got over that, he'd pick up a piece of food and just hold it. A few weeks later, he'd pick up the food and put it in his mouth, but wouldn't let go of it. He'd just suck on it until it was utterly obliterated. Finally, he learned. And I got down on my knees and thanked God.

As your babies get more skilled with foods, introduce the more complicated stuff. Some suggestions:

- Pancakes (Make a whole batch and freeze the leftovers. Just thaw them on subsequent days as needed.)
- Grilled cheese (Cut sandwiches into bite-size pieces.)
- Cheese sandwiches (ungrilled)
- Cubed turkey, ham, or cheese
- Cottage cheese
- Yogurt
- Macaroni and cheese (We spoon-feed this one!)
- Lasagna (If you are having a particularly brave day.)

Because the digestive system isn't fully mature at birth, Dr. Liberty recommends avoiding peanut butter, nuts of any kind, eggs, fish, and citrus fruits during the first year and maybe longer—depending on the individual child. Check with your pediatrician regarding any other foods you should avoid due to family allergies or other predispositions to possible allergies. These might include berries or whole wheat. The list will likely be small (unless you are Mollie, whose husband we call "bubble boy," because the poor thing has so many allergies), so you can use this time to experiment and see what your babies enjoy.

Also, be sure to avoid foods that pose a choking hazard to children less than three years of age. These include, but are not limited to:

- Raisins and other dried fruit
- Hard vegetables such as carrots
- Nuts
- Hot dogs
- Popcorn
- Chips
- Pretzels
- Grapes
- Hard candy
- Gum
- Jelly beans
- Whole corn kernels

One issue the sorority members struggled with during this food experimentation period was whether our babies were getting enough to eat. We knew two jars of commercial baby food or four frozen homemade baby food cubes were enough, but once we started putting a variety of diced food on their trays, were they eating until they were satisfied? Was their mid-afternoon meltdown a sign of extreme fatigue or extreme hunger?

When I asked Dr. Liberty about this, she commented how important regular visits to the pediatrician's office were to monitor the child's growth. Every infant is different. Some infants do very well with solids at six months, and others are slower to start. She cautions parents against forcing a spoon or food into their child's mouth. If the infant opens his or her mouth for food, seems interested and content, she recommends following those cues.

Most toddlers exhibit a decrease in appetite at around twelve to fifteen months because their growth and calorie needs change. Dr. Liberty recommends offering small (diced) bits of food with a good variety. Don't fill a toddler's plate; that can overwhelm children of this age, and they won't eat well. It's not uncommon for toddlers to eat only a few bites of each item.

She also cautions parents not to give toddlers frequent snacks between meals because that may suppress their appetite. This includes juice. The high sugar content is an appetite-killer, and juice (even fruit juice) is not very nutritious. Toddlers may need three to five small meals per day, so it's best to keep meals/snacks nutritious. Most children under age three don't eat for any reason other than hunger (unlike their mothers who often eat out of boredom alone). If your babies are cranky and accepting food, they are likely hungry.

Additionally, Dr. Liberty recommends that families eat together when possible because children learn their eating habits from their parents. Now, I practically had a coronary after hearing this. Our kitchen table only seated four. The boys normally ate before David got home, and Grace often ate next to me as I tended to a baby or with David while I readied the boys for bed. I would then down my infamous Rice Krispies dinner around 8:00 p.m. while David complained about how hungry he was. Needless to say, we felt horrible for Grace and knew the dinner hour provided a great opportunity to talk as a family, so we invested in a larger table. (At this stage, Jack and Henry were often excused from the formal dinner ritual.)

Once the babies get closer to a year of age, they may need (read: want) a small snack after their afternoon nap. Be wary of giving them large snacks, as that will prevent them from wanting much to eat during the dinner hour. But a small snack to tide them over (and give them something productive to do for twenty minutes) is not necessarily a bad idea.

The ability to choose their own snack may become appealing. One way Kristi handled it was to keep airtight, stackable storage containers on the counter. She kept them filled with crackers, cheerios, and other snack items, and they were only an arm's reach away when she needed them.

We put different snack choices (small bags of cheerios, Gerber Graduates fruit puffs or veggie puffs, Gerber

Graduates cookies and crackers, or other small wafer-like crackers) in small Tupperware containers. We offered each baby a choice between two portion-controlled containers for each snack. When they were finished, the container went into the dishwasher and was refilled the next day.

DEEP-SIXING BOTTLES

Anyone who uses the phrase "easy as taking candy from a baby" has never tried taking candy from a baby.

—Author Unknown

At some point during this six- to twelve-month timeframe (likely toward the latter end), you'll want to introduce sippy cups to your babies. They may want nothing to do with them for some time. With my daughter, we ended up switching her cold turkey the day after her first birthday. My pediatrician warned me that she might not consume any liquids for an entire day to make us feel bad enough to give back her bottle. It was a long day, and she did a lot of screaming. But by the next day, she took that sippy cup and never looked back.

With the boys, I offered sippy cups of water during their feedings when they were about seven months old. Many times, they'd only touch them. Other times, they'd throw them on the floor. I wasn't worried whether they drank from them or not, I just wanted the boys to get used to them. When I offered them sips, Henry would drink from the cup, but only if I held it; Jack just chewed on it. Neither option portended long-term success, but I realized patience was the key. By eleven months of age, both babies drank out of the sippy cups—when they wanted to—and I knew when we threw the bottles out, they'd be thirsty and use the cups.

Many people buy a certain brand of sippy cups, and when their babies don't sip right away, worry that it's the spout or the particular brand of cup that's too hard to suck from. They then consider trying another sippy cup. I have been one of these people. I have owned at least one of every brand and style of sippy cup on the market—handles, no handles, spill-proof spout, no spill-proof spout, rounded cup, straighter cup, you name it. My advice to you is this: if you think the issue is the type of sippy cup, try *one* other brand/style. If they sip with that one, while it may be coincidence, pat yourself on the back and proclaim that you knew it all along. If they don't sip, do *not* go and buy another variety. Before you know it, you'll have every brand and style on your cupboard shelf, and more than likely, your babies will sip from none of them. Or, they'll take to a newer one, but give them the other brands, and they'll more than likely sip from those, too—they just figured out how to sip, that's all!

NEW CAR SEATS—AGAIN

Change is inevitable—except from a vending machine.
—Robert C. Gallagher

Sometime during this period, you'll switch from the infant car seats (if that's what you started with) to the convertible rear-facing/front-facing car seats. Remember, your babies *must* face backward until they are one year old *and* twenty pounds. An infant's neck isn't strong enough to handle a head-on collision, and the damage to the developing brain is severe if the head forcibly snaps forward.

Twenty pounds is recommended for proper fit of the harness in the larger car seats. I know that getting your babies in and out of those backward-facing car seats, especially if they're in the back row of a van or large SUV, is a nightmare that prompts vivid dreams of weekly visits to a licensed massage therapist, but it's worth it for their safety.

There are so many car seats to choose from. Our recommendation is, find one that not only face backward, but has a tether strap to further secure the seat in your vehicle. These tethers are amazing and make your car seat fit so tightly in your car that you feel it's part of the vehicle.

Installing these seats backwards, however, is no small feat. If you try and try and sweat and sweat and still are not comfortable with the fit, call your local police station—like you did with the infant car seats—and ask to make an appointment to have your car seat installed. Note that, while not required, the car seat checkers who perform on-site inspections at stores such as Babies "R" Us often want your babies to be with you so they can verify how you buckle your babies in, which is as important as how tightly your car seat is installed.

THE LUCRATIVE GARAGE SALE

The ad in the paper said, "Big sale. Last week." Why advertise? I already missed it. They're just rubbing it in.

—Yakov Smirnoff

There comes a point during the first year when you suddenly realize how much stuff you have accumulated that is no longer being used: infant car seats, infant clothes, swings, bouncy seats, Boppy Pillows, the list goes on and on. If you plan to have other children—in fact, if you think there is even the remote possibility you will have another child—I encourage you to find a nice spot somewhere in the recesses of your basement to stow all this stuff until you need it again. If, on the other hand, you are of my mindset, and have declared that only by an act of God will you ever bear children again, there are easy (and profitable) ways to rid yourself of all this stuff.

The first place that will help you get rid of all this stuff, one the entire sorority found the most profitable, is eBay. Early on, I encouraged you to hold onto the original boxes the gear came in so, if you chose to sell it, you'd have an easier time packing it than if you had to start from scratch. If you didn't heed my advice or, for some other reason, no longer possess those boxes, it's okay. You can improvise or decide to rid yourself of those bigger items via other means.

eBay is a great place to sell baby equipment because it goes fast, and you almost always profit from it more than you would through a garage sale. I have no idea why. With shipping, many folks pay close to the cost of a new piece of equipment, but I say, don't spend a lot of time questioning the actions of perfect strangers.

Another method is to hold a garage sale. Mollie and I did just that when our babies were about nine months old. Garage sales are great for getting rid of baby clothes, because the time required to photograph and list all those clothes on eBay won't pay off financially in the end unless you sell the clothes in large lots by size. Most folks buying clothing on eBay are looking for items advertised as NWT (New With Tags).

Garage sales are another great way to get rid of bigger items. If you advertise "baby" in the garage sale ad, people come running. If you advertise "mother of twins" or "multiple mothers of twins," as we did, you'll have an even better turnout. I rid my basement of an infant car seat and coordinating stroller through this sale that I wouldn't have attempted to sell on eBay. For one thing, I had no idea how to package it, and for another, it would've cost about $200 to ship.

PLAYING TOGETHER (OR NOT)

I always laugh the hardest at the stuff you see in day-to-day life. It's great when somebody can tell a joke that really makes you laugh hard, but to see some kind of personal interaction that no one could write is so good. Those are always the things that make me laugh.

—Luke Wilson

Within this six- to twelve-month timeframe, your babies will likely start to interact more and more. Be prepared; it may not be in the most positive way, but that needn't matter. The key is that they realize the other exists. If they have fun battering each other, at least they are entertaining one another, albeit temporarily.

Jack and Henry's first real interaction wasn't so nice. Henry was ultra-dependent on his pacifiers, and Jack seemed to know this. At eight months of age, he reached through the crib slats into Henry's crib, stole the pacifier right out of Henry's mouth, and chewed on it. As you can imagine, Henry had a fit, and it required intervention. As time went on, however, they enjoyed playing tug-of-war with toys and talking to each other more and more (in a language I didn't understand in the least). They worked together to stack blocks (and then knock them down), roll balls from one end of the room to the other, and occasionally watched TV sitting right up against one another or with one's hand on top of the other's. Seeing multiples interact with one another, in fact, is one of the greatest joys of raising them.

Kristi kept two Pack 'n Plays in their family room situated right next to each other. Each is filled with toys. She put a child in each one, and they had fun playing with the toys in their respective Pack 'n Play as well as handing toys back and forth. There was an occasional brawl over a toy or two, but overall they enjoyed their time, and Kristi was able to get some other household duties completed.

GETTING AWAY: THE FAMILY ROAD TRIP

Sure, give me an adventure and I'll ride it.

—Melissa Auf der Maur

Likely, during this period, there will come a time when you think to yourself, "I don't care where we go, but we *have* to get out of this town for a day or two." You'll probably debate whether loading up everyone and everything is worth getting those days away. But more likely, you won't even stop to think about the logistics, because you'll be in such need of getting away!

Believe me, this is doable. Holly and Paul headed out one Friday to go camping for the weekend with their ten-month-old triplets. I thought they'd lost their minds. Not only did they pack up the necessities—bottles, formula, food, clothes—they packed two exersaucers, bouncy seats, maybe even a swing, I don't know. They had a blast. They were so relieved to be away from home, they didn't even think about the inconvenience. And they swear to this day that the girls were so excited to be in a new environment, they slept better and seemed happier than they'd been in quite some time.

When our boys were about nine months old, we headed to my parents' house for Memorial Day weekend. We followed Mollie and Gary, who went to Mollie's parents' house. Their drive was about nine hours; ours was nearly fourteen. We followed each other for the first six hours or so, talking back and forth on walkie-talkies, and then split to go north and south, respectively. It was a great, although short, weekend, and the excitement of getting away made the long drive and frequent stops well worth it.

And, since we drove through the night, David and I had more successive hours just to talk about whatever we wanted than we'd had since the boys were born. (By the way, if the drive to your final destination is a long one, driving through the night is a very good idea. If you manage to stay awake, you can log several hours of driving time without having to stop to feed or change someone. But the ability to stay awake is obviously critical.)

You need not go on a long trip to feel you're away. Find a neat location within two or three hours of home and head there for the weekend. Preferably, find somewhere with a kid-friendly atmosphere, family restaurants, and places to walk. It doesn't work well to go somewhere with a largely adult crowd and a plethora of antique shops, for instance.

AIRLINE TRAVEL

I remember my wife and I used to get on a plane and see everybody else with their babies. They'd be putting strollers and car seats up above, and we'd think, "Oh, please, Lord, don't make us go through that."
—Paul Reiser

If just the thought of traveling on a plane with your kids makes you crazy, let alone traveling internationally, read on! With this helpful information in hand, you and your family really can survive a long-distance trip.

Regardless of whether it's for the first or fifty-first time, one can't help but laugh while watching Clark Griswold and his family endlessly and hopelessly circle Big Ben and Parliament in *National Lampoon's European Vacation*. However, when imagining their own crew in the same situation, most parents' laughter quickly turns to nauseating anxiety.

Traveling by air with twins under the age of, well, twelve can seem a daunting proposition. In fact, after thirty or so seconds of consideration, many parents likely decide to simplify their adventures by heading for the shores of the continent on which they reside (or perhaps simply to the Holiday Inn just down the road).

I don't know any families who dreamt of taking a European vacation with twins under the age of one, however, I do know families who have relatives living in other countries. It was important to them to introduce their babies to these relatives, particularly if the relatives were unable to travel to the United States.

According to Amie O'Shaughnessy, founder of Ciao Bambino, a travel service that specializes in helping parents travel to Italy with children (and soon other European destinations as well), "The biggest misconception parents have about international travel with young children is that it is just too hard. Parents fear that, after a long flight, they will experience a relocation—more work in a new place—and struggle to find basic resources in a foreign environment."

With proper planning, this fallacy can be avoided. Notes O'Shaughnessy, "If itineraries and destinations are chosen with care, resources are easily accessible, including first-rate pediatric medical care, high quality accommodations with kitchens, baby supplies, equipment, and interesting activities for the entire family."

Whether heading for the local amusement park or the Louvre, the importance of effective preparation cannot be overlooked. It can undeniably set the stage for a wonderful experience or a Never Again nightmare.

A valid concern for families considering a trip with young children is the potential for a child to fall ill days before departure. O'Shaughnessy's recommendation: "Families should purchase travel insurance (which can be done easily over the Internet) to cover money that may be lost due to trip changes and cancellations. In addition, parents need to confirm [that] their existing medical insurance plan covers international travel, and carry a list of relevant contact numbers."

While we have yet to travel internationally with our children, we have traveled domestically by plane several times. In the midst of packing ten suitcases, corralling our herd to the car, and strategizing how we'll get through security without delaying the entire line for two hours, the number of things my husband and I are likely to inadvertently leave behind when embarking on any trip is astounding. My mantra has become: "As long as I have my driver's license and my credit card, anything else can be purchased en route."

For international ventures, however, a few more items must be accounted for before heading to the airport. All children, including babies, are required to have a passport when traveling internationally. Additionally, if one parent intends to travel with her child, but without her spouse, she must have a letter from her spouse (preferably notarized) stating that it is acceptable to take the child out of the country.

Next on the list of importance, after a passport and a credit card, are supplies. "Although a wide range of baby supplies can be readily purchased when traveling outside the United States, I advise parents to bring products with them when the specific brand and ingredients are important," notes O'Shaughnessy. My friend, Cindy, who traveled to Italy with her 10-month-old twins, agreed. "Thank goodness I brought enough food, because their selection of baby food was much different from ours."

There's nothing worse than setting off on a much-anticipated adventure only to have the children begin complaining before the pilot has had a chance to welcome you on board. Choose the contents of your carry-on bags carefully. Doing so will go a long way toward avoiding the type of meltdown that might have you wondering when the flight attendants will begin serving "adult beverages."

Advises Sarah Sims, who frequently travels to England with her two young sons, "Have a backpack for each child. Stash snacks in each bag in the event of an unforeseen delay. And put all bottles, sippy cups, and other liquids in their own Ziploc® bag with a paper towel. If something spills or leaks due to pressure changes, changes of clothing and other items aren't ruined."

In light of the ever-changing FDA rules and regulations regarding what travelers can and cannot take on board in their carry-on bags, be sure to check the current rules a few days before your departure.

Many parents wonder whether they should take their child's car seat on the plane. Urges Sims, "Don't bother; check them instead. They are a pain to get to the plane, into the seat, and off again. Children under two (who typically do not require their own seat) can usually be put into a bassinet or special seat provided by the airline and attached to the bulkhead wall. If you do plan to bring a car seat for a child under two, check first with the airline for their requirements."

Cindy recommends wearing layers on the plane so that if your child spits up (or empties the entire contents of his stomach onto your shirt seven minutes after takeoff), you can simply remove it and reveal a clean one underneath.

If traveling with older children who aren't likely to throw a tantrum in the terminal—professing their need to go home for the stuffed animal they haven't looked at for three years—don't overlook the importance of keeping them occupied for several hours—not to mention through potential delays. Ensuring that each child has a backpack filled with a variety of activities can mean the difference between a patient traveler and never-ending barrage of "Are we there yet?"

It often works well to individually wrap several items such as sticker books, coloring books, and Doodle pads, and stick them in your child's backpack. Allow him to open a new item at certain intervals along the way. That way, his entertainment is spaced out, and he doesn't find himself void of things to do after only thirteen minutes in the air.

One issue parents often don't address until they have no choice—because their children are bouncing off the walls at 3:00 in the morning and zonked at noon—is jet lag. Proposes Sims, "If you are dealing with a time change, start feeding and napping kids according to your destination's local time once you board the aircraft, and incorporate as much of their regular routine as possible." If your twins are much younger than six months, their schedules may more readily accommodate a time change (because they don't yet *have* a regular schedule!).

If you have family at your destination, inquire as to whether they can obtain Pack 'n Plays, travel cribs, highchairs, and any other equipment you might need on the other end. The goal is to pack as little as possible beyond the necessities, which will take up quite enough space in and of themselves.

While parents will likely fall with a long sigh of relief into their own beds after returning home, they shouldn't expect their children to have exactly the same reaction. "It took about three weeks to get back on schedule," remembers Cindy. "The babies adjusted to the time change within about two days when we arrived in Italy, but it took about five days when we returned home." Obviously, for domestic travel, it (hopefully) won't take quite this long for babies to get back on their regular schedule.

The best thing parents can do to help their kids get back on schedule after a trip is to get them back into their own routine *immediately*. Even if children don't take to it right away, parents should begin operating under their previous schedule as soon as possible. (It will help parents assimilate as well!)

So, whether you have relatives in foreign lands or not, perhaps you should forget the standard vacation this year. Instead of a walk on a familiar beach, give some thought to a stroll along the Great Wall of China, the Seine, or maybe even around Big Ben and Parliament (just once). I mean, hey, at this point, what's a little more insanity?

THE MIRACLE OF SELF-SUFFICIENCY

Freedom is a possession of inestimable value.

—Cicero

I swear, the greatest joy I felt that first year—next to realizing I had just slept for eight hours without interruption—was the sight of Jack holding his own bottle. If the neighbors had seen my happy dance when I noticed this feat, they surely would have concluded that they lived next to a complete weirdo.

Jack accomplished this about two weeks before Henry and about four weeks after Olivia and Kambria. (I had to beg Barb not to mention that the girls were eating, because I knew that meant they were doing so independently, while Barb was doing something else. In my house, I was still a slave to holding the boys' bottles.)

Jack holding his bottle felt like instant freedom. I thought to myself: Imagine the possibilities. I can mix and give the boys their bottles at 5:00 a.m. without sitting and holding them for thirty minutes. If I'm worried about them choking, I can sit in a chair and read! Or, I can hand them their bottles, change their diapers as they drink, and then go back to bed. (Luckily, my boys didn't fall asleep while drinking their bottles; they just threw them out of their cribs when they were finished. I knew I'd probably pay for this luxury somewhere down the line, but at the time, I wasn't worried about it!)

I can have them drink their bottles, I thought, as I make dinner. I can give them bottles in their car seats while I'm driving and not have to stop in the parking lot of some grocery store, squeeze my understandably huge hips between the car seats, and give my arms the workout of their lives while they drink slower than molasses flows in winter.

If your babies aren't able yet to hold their own bottles, be patient. This skill usually emerges quite suddenly. Who knows, it could happen tomorrow!

GIFT CLOTHES: OUTGROWN

Clothes make the man. Naked people have little or no influence on society.

—Mark Twain

During Holly and Paul's triplets' first year of life, they dressed them in the most adorable, coordinated outfits I've ever seen. One lovely spring day they all emerged from their van, and the girls were in sleeveless gingham swing tops with bloomers underneath. One girl's outfit was yellow, one was purple, and one was pink. Each also had color-coordinated sneakers and hair bows. On another occasion, the girls all wore pinstriped stretch pants with coordinating sweaters. Each sweater had a different animal or flower on the front. They again had coordinating shoes and hair bows. Holly was so kind to ensure that each girl had "her color." This made it easier to identify which name belonged to which child, especially since two of the triplets are identical. The only caveat: we had to remember which color was whose!

Each time I commented on these outfits, Holly said they were a gift, and that Paul would have killed her if she'd purchased that many matching outfits. I just wondered when they were going to run out!

For most moms of multiples, however, the supply of gift clothes does run out at some point, and you are faced with purchasing not just one adorable pair of wide-wale corduroys with coordinating button-down shirt for your son, or a pair of tights covered with multi-colored butterflies for your daughter, but two (or more). This can feel prohibitive in a hurry. You find yourself saying over and over again, "If I only had to buy one of these, I could justify it, but *two*?"

One note about this: chances are, if you did buy only one, you'd still be deciding if you could justify it. I know this from birthing a singleton before twins. It's all perspective. I shudder to remember the days when I thought having one infant who slept eighteen hours a day was challenging and "interrupting my routine."

Some practical ways to get around this clothes-buying dilemma are to go garage-sale shopping, frequent second-hand children's shops, or borrow clothes from your friends.

When I had Grace, I swore up and down that I wouldn't

buy my kids' clothes at garage sales, but you wouldn't believe how nice some garage-sale clothes are! In affluent areas, people don't attempt to sell clothes unless they are in great shape. I have really lucked out, and I say with all sincerity that some of my favorite clothing items for my sons' first winter came straight from a trendy mom's high-quality garage sale.

With second-hand children's shops (yes, here I go again with an endorsement for second-hand shops), you have to pick and choose. Some don't require the same quality in the clothes they buy and resell, but there is one near my house— and I know of others elsewhere—that demand clothes be in nearly new condition when buying from sellers. The only downside of second-hand stores is that oftentimes, by the time the store has added its markup to the price required by the seller, it's actually cheaper to hit a good sale at Baby Gap. However, I have lucked out repeatedly at second-hand stores and been thrilled with my finds.

Another fabulous solution our little "multiples" sorority developed was borrowing clothes from each other when our kids weren't wearing the same sizes. Mollie's boys are five weeks younger than Jack and Henry, but have always been smaller. They were still in size 6-12 months clothes while Jack and Henry were wearing size 12-18 months. So, all the gifts Mollie received for the winter in a 12-18 month size hung in my boys' closet for a while. As my kids outgrew them, hers grew into them. Since we lived then in the Midwest, it was undoubtedly always snowing in April, so her kids still got plenty of use out of the items. (So, all of you who bought 12-18 month winter outfits for Mollie's children need not feel bad; you clothed four kids instead of two.)

Another option is to ask stores whether they offer a twin discount. Many outlet stores offer a 10 percent discount above and beyond their already low prices. A few stores are gracious enough to offer this discount not only to parents of twins, but to grandparents of twins as well. Some establishments offer a discount on anything except sale merchandise. In recent years, certain stores have realized they are actually *losing* money by giving discounts to mothers of twins because so many twins are being born. Therefore, such stores have revamped their multiples discount to apply only to triplets and beyond. Nevertheless, it's always worth checking.

A final strategy: shop a season in advance. It can sometimes be challenging to guess what size your children might be in the following year, but in most cases you can determine if you'll be looking at 12-18 month clothes or 18-24 month clothes based on your children's size. If you keep your eyes open for end-of-season sales, it's possible to find deals so good you'll wonder if you're dreaming!

Once your babies are walking, a great deal is available on adorable, flexible shoes for little ones at Preschoolians™ (http://www.preschoolians.com). This company offers a 40 percent discount off your entire order if you have twins. You simply need to mail them a photo of your twins and request the discount. They send you a code you can use from that point forward when ordering.

WALKING

The finest inheritance you can give to a child is to allow it to make its own way, completely on its own feet.

—Isadora Duncan

This is an activity that may or may not surface by the time your kids reach twelve months of age. I froze stiff when I looked into my dining room (a.k.a. the toy room) and saw Jack standing up in the middle of the room with no support whatsoever. I whispered over and over, "Sit down, Jack. Just slowly…sit…down." Granted, he was thirteen months old when this occurred, but my point is, if it hasn't happened yet, it's on the horizon, so prepare yourself.

Some of the positives of your children learning to walk (since every stranger you bump into will proclaim the negatives) are: They'll be able to walk on short outings. They'll soon climb into the car and maybe even into their car seats. They'll walk where you need them to go (even though they're probably already crawling there, but hey, I'm just trying to point out the positives here).

Try not to be too nervous when your children are learning to walk and are a bit unsteady. They are going to fall now and then. Some kids practice for several months before walking a longer distance, taking one or two steps before falling, while others seemingly wait until they've perfected the activity in their heads and just stand up and start walking around the house. Grace did this, and David and I watched from the couch as though our child was possessed. It can be a bit odd to suddenly see your child vertically mobile after she's been sitting or lying down for her entire life!

Not too long ago, I was mindlessly paging through a catalog, and as I turned the page I did a double-take; I could not believe what I saw. The company was advertising a helmet for a child to wear while he's learning to walk. The theory was that if he fell, he wouldn't hurt himself if he was wearing a helmet. First there were knee pads to protect crawlers. Now there are helmets to protect walkers. Really, people, what's next? Full-body padding?

It's true that new walkers aren't terribly steady, but they aren't walking fast enough to do enough damage, should they fall, to require wearing a helmet. If your coffee table has sharp corners, or your family room is two steps down from your kitchen, or there's another object your child could hurt himself on should he fall, remove it, gate it off, or pad it until he's steadier. Frankly, depending on how much this helmet weighs, I wonder if it would make a kid top heavy and actually *cause* him to fall!

Remember that the best way for your children to learn to walk is with bare feet. There's no reason for you to spend a lot of money on special "new walker" shoes or any other shoes for them to walk in while inside. For outdoor excursions, if they're going to be in a stroller and won't pull their socks off, keeping them in socks is fine. If they will be out and about on foot, reference my endorsement of Preschoolians™ shoes (and the associated twins' discount) on page 222.

THE DESIRE TO RETURN TO WORK

I have an office in my house and one about five minutes from my house. I worked solely out of my house for many years, but find, with children, that I have to be in a different zip code to think.

—Cathy Guisewite

Many new moms of twins return to work either for financial reasons or because their job is part of what defines them, and they are uncomfortable parting with that aspect of their life. As I mentioned early on, if you plan to go back to work after your babies are born, be sure to research your childcare options early in your pregnancy. I know several people who were shocked to find that some reputable daycare facilities in their area had a waitlist of up to six months.

If you plan to explore the nanny or au pair option, careful planning is again the key. Many nanny or au pair placement agencies require several months to process an application, conduct interviews, and establish final placement. It's wise to get this process under way before you near the end of your pregnancy, because, with two babies on the way, you never know exactly when the end will be!

Not every woman has to return to work immediately after her babies are born. Some are fortunate enough to stay at home with their babies if they choose. However, if you opt to be a stay-at-home mom, "I think I need to go back to work" is a phrase you are likely to utter more than a few times during this time period. The reason? You're tired of a few things.

Possible Reasons for Wanting to Return to Work

You're Exhausted

You'll be convinced (and possibly rightly so) that it would be easier physically and mentally to be a garbage man dumping fifty-pound trashcans, or a construction worker building eighty-story buildings all day, than doing what you are doing.

You're Bored

Well, "bored" is a bad word to use when you're discussing raising twins. What I mean is, you get tired of not having adults to converse with all day long. You're concerned that one day, you might find yourself having a professional conversation with someone in that high-pitched "I'm-talking-to-a-baby" voice.

You're Hungry

You're tired of hearing about the delicious meal your husband had for lunch.

You Think You're Losing Brain Cells

You're convinced that you're getting dumber by the second from not using your intellect very often anymore. (I have a stack of *New York Times* crossword puzzles—granted, in a drawer—that I have pledged to do just to keep my brain fine-tuned.)

For the record, it's been shown that a woman's brain shrinks by anywhere from 2 to 8 percent of its original size during pregnancy. Researchers believe this is due to the developing baby's need for lipids. The brain is made up of 60 percent fat, and is rich in DHA (docosahexaenoic acid; try to say that three times quickly).

DHA is critical for the development of a baby's eyes and brain, most importantly during the last trimester of pregnancy. At this late stage, DHA is so important to the developing baby that if the placenta can't extract the proper amount to support the needs of the developing baby (or babies) from the mother's blood supply, the DHA is obtained from the mother's brain.[4]

Sadly, women can't use this phenomenon indefinitely to excuse their conviction that they're losing their minds. The brain appears to return to its normal size about six months after delivery.

My question is, if you're carrying two babies, does that mean your brain shrinks by 16 percent? Somehow, I doubt it. But it sure would explain a few things. And, while I can't prove it, I think it's highly probable that my brain did *not* return to its original size after pregnancy. Perhaps after the birth of all four of our children, it just got confused and stayed shrunk. Yep, I think that's it.

You Think Your Kids Need Some Variety

You've convinced yourself that your kids are getting sick of your presence and are never going to obey the word, "No," or the phrase, "Please don't…" regardless of how nicely you say them.

Any of that sound familiar? I contemplated returning to work no fewer than 197 times before the boys turned one year old. Sometimes I was serious and other times not so serious. Luckily, I have an incredibly supportive husband who told me that, if I needed or wanted to go back to work, he would stand behind me 100 percent.

With three children, I could make $60,000 a year and practically lose money to place them in formal daycare. I also wanted to keep them in their own environment; that was very important to me. That meant finding a nanny. To pay the costs to search for and then employ a nanny, I had to have a well-paying job. To work that job, I had to have a nanny. Plus, embarking on the tedious process of finding a nanny we'd be happy with wasn't terribly appealing. Even as a mother of multiples, there were too many logistics to coordinate at once. As you can see, there's great benefit in researching childcare options early.

When the boys were nearly one-year-old, my friend Stephanie, who had babysat for the boys early on and then left her full-time job to get her Masters in Education, offered to quit her part-time job and work for me three days a week as a nanny. I was so elated I thought I would burst. I knew Stephanie well, she was fabulous with my kids, and my kids loved her. What more could you ask for in a nanny?

So, I sent out my résumé left and right. And I didn't send them out blindly. I sent them in response to job postings on popular job-posting Internet sites; supposedly these were legitimate positions companies were looking to hire someone for. Even though some of the positions were a stretch, many of them seemed a perfect fit with my background—or at least close enough to garner a phone call! But nothing happened. I never heard from anyone.

After spending a few hours wondering how I had become so completely worthless to corporate America, I decided perhaps I wasn't yet ready to return to working outside the house. In the course of this multiples-rearing thing, I found myself having to turn my life over to fate. It took some of the burden off me, anyway. I thought, "Maybe—even though I'm ready to pull my hair out—at this point the place where I am of most value is here in this house with these children." If the right opportunity had presented itself, I would still have considered it, but it had to be suitable for me and for my family. Therefore, I decided to continue relishing the opportunity to help my kids grow and develop and learn to say, "Please."

My friends Sonya, Jean, and Holly all work full-time. I think that more than wanting or needing the money, they enjoy working. Sonya could not only be CEO of her household, she could be CEO of the planet. She's extremely intelligent, focused, and driven. She spent many years building her professional credentials, and she wanted that dynamic to continue to be part of her life after her twins were born. Sonya's husband, Bob, retired from his job as an airline pilot to be the boys' primary caregiver.

Jean is an accountant, and also loves her job. The arrangement that worked best for Jean and her husband was to find a caregiver who could provide daycare for their twins in her home with a few other children.

Holly worked full-time for a few months after their triplets were born. Her job was the type that never ended. She was on call virtually 24/7. The only thing that made her job different from being a mother was that there weren't any kids in the office! At some point, she decided that particular job wasn't right for her any longer. But of all the determined women I've met, if any of them *needs* to have at least twenty balls in the air at one time, it's Holly (and she juggles the balls so gracefully, you'd never know they were there). Since leaving her full-time job, she's taken on many part-time opportunities doing things she enjoys from her home.

I remember watching an interview with Cindy Crawford shortly after she had her first child. She was asked whether the fair amount of criticism she got for returning to work after her son was born had bothered her. She responded by saying she was a person who *had* to work to some degree. She had cut back considerably, she said, but, to be a good mother to her son, she had to do something other than just stay at home with him all day long. It was how she stayed sane and focused. I think that's highly respectable.

Once they have children, women are still sometimes criticized for working if they don't need to for financial reasons. But the bottom line is, you have to do what you have to do to be the best mom you can be. And if that includes working two or three or five days a week, part-time or full-time, then that's what you have to do. At the end of the day, both you and your children will be better for it.

So, if you start to feel the "I've-gotta-go-back" bug, explore it. See what your options are. If an appealing opportunity presents itself, give it a try. What do you have to lose? I know several women who work at their local department store two nights and one weekend day a week to earn some extra spending money (and a store discount) and get away from the house for a few hours. They love it!

There are definitely options beyond working one hundred hours per week. You must simply determine what works best for you and your family, and find something that accommodates those parameters.

FIVE

Happy Birthday!

Happiness is different from pleasure. Happiness has something to do with struggling and enduring and accomplishing.

—George Sheehan

You did it! Wasn't so bad, was it? When Jack and Henry turned one, people asked over and over, "Can you believe they're a year old already?" I didn't know how to answer that question. Time certainly does fly, but when I thought back to the day they were born, it seemed like ten years had elapsed. Each day can feel like a lifetime, but each year also feels like a day.

As I finish this book, Grace is three and a half years old and the boys nearly fifteen months. The boys wrestle with each other. They steal from each other. They push each other. They cannot go to sleep at night unless the other is within eyesight. Jack calls Henry "Bobba." The other day, Jack went over and sat on Henry's lap (and Henry had a complete fit). They speak their own language (and I shudder to think what they are saying about me). And the best is yet to come—potty training, preschool, ballet lessons, drivers' licenses, college…

As I close, I have several wishes for you: May you feel blessed every day. May you eat a good, warm meal at least once a week. May you have an amazing group of supportive friends and family who make you laugh when you most need to. I can promise you one thing: this sorority is with you every diaper, bottle, and step of the way.

Appendix A

Making Your Own Baby Food

As I mentioned earlier, making your own baby food couldn't be easier. With a toddler running around in addition to my twins, I would have been the first to admit it, had it been too much. Remember, I'm the one who returned the hospital-grade breast pump after the first rental month because I couldn't find time to pump. So, if I'm saying you can do this, you can do this!

To reiterate, there's nothing wrong with commercial baby food. It's convenient and the serving sizes are prepared ahead of time. But it's expensive, and, as I learned after making my own food, it has limitations when it comes to variety and the combinations the manufacturers have chosen. I mean, plums and tapioca? Enough said. In addition, commercially prepared baby food often contains more water, starch, and sugar than homemade baby food.

There are some simple supplies you should have on hand before you begin:

- Food processor
- Food mill
- Steamer basket
- Ice cube trays
- Sandwich bags
- Gallon-size freezer bags

PRELIMINARIES

Some simple rules regarding food safety should be followed when making your own baby food:

- Be sure to wash your hands and your tools thoroughly before making your babies' food to ensure that no germs or other contaminants are introduced into the food.

- Do not let cooked food come into contact with raw food to reduce the likelihood of bacterial contamination.

- Do not let baby food sit at room temperature for more than two hours. After this point, bacteria begins to grow. Refrigerate or freeze the food as soon as possible after preparing it.

Step-by-Step

1. Wash hands and equipment well with hot, soapy water.

2. Wash fruits and vegetables and remove skin, if desired, and seeds. I occasionally left skins on after scrubbing them really well. If you have a good food mill, the skins will either be left behind or become so ground up that your babies won't even notice they are there.

3. Bake, boil, or steam food until tender.

4. Use a food mill, blender, food processor, or fork to mash food until smooth.

5. If necessary, add liquid (water, formula, or breast milk) to thin out thick foods. I also believe adding formula or breast milk to food you'll freeze helps it thaw with a

creamier texture as opposed to a freeze-dried texture.

6. Pour food you'll use in the next twenty-four hours into a bowl in the refrigerator; put the remainder into ice cube trays. Cover filled ice cube trays with plastic wrap and put them in the freezer for a day or so until the cubes are frozen. Pop the cubes out and put them into a large, labeled, and dated freezer bag.

7. When you want to use cubes from the freezer, put the number you wish to thaw in a bowl in the refrigerator or microwave them for a few seconds. You don't need the food to be too warm; it only needs to be at about room temperature. If using the microwave, be sure to stir the food *very* well to eliminate hot spots. Also, test the temperature of the food before offering it to your babies.

BABY FOOD RECIPES:
THE BASICS

*NOTE: These foods are listed in the approximate order in which most of us offered them to our babies. There's no right or wrong approach in the order you choose. It's a commonly held belief that it's a good idea to offer vegetables before fruits because fruit will give your babies a taste for sweeter foods, and then they may not be interested in the vegetables. I know people who have started with fruits, however, and done just fine.

Storage Times

Food	In Refrigerator	In Freezer
Fruits and Vegetables	1-2 days	2 months
Meats or Egg Yolks	1 day	2 months

Meat/Veggie Combo   1-2 days   2 months

Fruits

Peaches

Remove pit and slice peaches into wedges. Steam peaches until they are extremely soft. (Steaming helps to keep the vitamins in the food; if you boil the fruit, you will lose more of the vitamins in the water.) Use a food mill to purée them. The skins will either be ground up so fine into the peach mixture that you won't notice them, or they'll stay behind in the food mill. The food will likely be so watery that you won't need to add any breast milk or formula to it. If you need to add some liquid, use the liquid in the bottom of the steamer. It has plenty of vitamins from the peaches. Put the peaches in ice cube trays and freeze.

Pears

Follow instructions above.

Plums

Follow instructions above.

Bananas

I usually waited until the bananas were extremely ripe and then mashed them with a fork to the desired consistency. When combining bananas with another fruit or vegetable, mash the desired quantity and stir in with the other food before transferring the food into ice cube trays. Remember not to combine bananas with other foods until you know the baby can tolerate the food to which you are adding the bananas.

Vegetables

Green Beans

Frozen green beans are the easiest to use. We also found them (along with peas) to be the least desirable to the babies. Steam the green beans until they are extremely soft and then purée them in a food processor. If your babies don't take to the green beans, try mixing them with a sweeter vegetable you have already tried, such as sweet potatoes or squash, or mix them with a fruit once you have ensured that your babies can tolerate it.

Peas

Again, frozen works best here. Steam the peas until they are very soft, then purée them in a food processor. As with green beans, if your babies don't like peas, try mixing them with sweet potatoes or squash, or mix them with a fruit once you have ensured that your babies tolerate it.

Sweet Potatoes

Pierce four to five sweet potatoes with the tines of a fork and microwave them for approximately 25 minutes on high. Alternatively, bake them in the oven at 375°F for an hour to an hour and a half. Scoop out the flesh and blend it, along with an ounce or two of formula or breast milk, in a food processor. Continue adding breast milk or formula until it's creamy. Spoon into ice cube trays and freeze.

Squash

Cut several butternut squash in half. (We tried a variety of squash and found that butternut works best.) There's no need to add butter or brown sugar to the squash, unless, of course, you plan to eat one yourself for dinner! The squash is plenty sweet on its own for the babies' tastes. Cook the squash at 350°F for 45 minutes to an hour, until the flesh is soft. Scoop out the flesh and blend it along with an ounce or two of formula or breast milk in a food processor. Continue adding breast milk or formula until it's creamy. Spoon into ice cube trays and freeze.

Meats

Truth be told, none of us actually made our own puréed meat. The texture (and smell) of it didn't particularly agree with the babies or frankly, with the adults! Once our babies were old enough (around eight or nine months of age), we offered shredded meat or meat diced into small pieces. Success was also found through putting chicken breasts or a roast in the Crockpot, cooking for six to eight hours, and then shredding. You easily add flavor to the meat this way, which makes it far more appealing.

Many of us discovered that our babies wanted nothing to do with meats until they were closer to fourteen months old, whether it was shredded, diced, or puréed. To ensure that they were getting adequate protein until then, we offered them cheese, beans, yogurt, and other protein-rich foods. Ruth Yaron also shares great ideas in her book for protein alternatives such as tofu.

Once you know your babies will tolerate a variety of the above foods, combine them! I made batches of plums and sweet potatoes, or bananas and pears, or a combination of three or more. The more foods you combine, the larger the batch, which is helpful if you run low on food and need to make a big batch of *something*. It's easier to make a big batch of pears, bananas, and green beans than it is to make separate batches of each of those and combine them later.

If your babies don't enjoy green beans or peas as much as you'd like, make a batch of pears and add a small amount of green beans or peas. The sweetness of the fruit may persuade them to eat it, and they'll still be getting a healthy serving of vegetables without really knowing it.

References

1. Yokoyama, Y. Comparison of child-rearing problems between mothers with multiple children who conceived after infertility treatment and mothers with multiple children who conceived spontaneously. *Twin Res.* 2003;6:89-96

2. Thorpe K, Golding J, MacGillivray I, Greenwood R. Comparison of prevalence of depression in mothers of twins and mothers of singletons. BMJ 1991;302:875-7

3. Beck CT. Releasing the pause button: mothering twins during the first year of life. *Qual Health Res.* 2002;12:593-608

4. Brewer, S. DHA - Brain Food. *Healthspan* 2003

Index